Always Springtime

Other Books by Author—

The Education of Sisters (1940)
Then and Now (1946)
Devotedly Yours (1950)
A Woman Named Louise (1956)
Sisters for the 21st Century (1965)
Always Springtime (1969)

DEDICATION

For Sister Catherine herself
because there is absolutely
nobody on earth like her

and

For all the Sisters in the
world, with her love, because
that is the way she would
have wanted it.

ALWAYS SPRINGTIME

Sister Bertrande Meyers, D.C.

President Emeritus, Marillac College
Saint Louis, Missouri

Biography of a woman who
was not born a saint, but who
became one by a do-it-yourself method.

MARILLAC TOWERS PRESS

7800 Natural Bridge Road
Saint Louis, Missouri
63121

ACKNOWLEDGMENTS

To

Sister Mary Rose McPhee
Who made this book possible

and to her Secretary

Sister Margaret Mary O'Connor,
Our Reference Book for Dates, Statistics

To

Sister Mary Meehan
Who saved (and sent us)

Letters received from Sister Catherine

Over a period of 39 years

To

Mr. Joseph Sullivan
and his wife, Ruby

For supplying family details

To

Mrs. Lucille O'Connell
A classmate of Sister Catherine's

For childhood memories

To

Sister Marie Sheehy
and

Mrs. Georgia Casey
Who typed and proofread the manuscript

and to all

Who sent notes and anecdotes

To these I tender my sincerest gratitude

SISTER BERTRANDE

FOREWORD

Our Lord states in the Gospel: "You are the light of the world . . . . No one lights a lamp to put it under a bushel; they put it on the lamp-stand where it shines for everyone in the house. In the same way your light must shine in the sight of men, so that, seeing your good works, they may give praise to your Father in heaven."

This quotation seems to apply in a special way to the life of Sister Catherine Sullivan, so fittingly symbolized in a flame which gives forth both light and warmth. In the sixty years of her dedicated life, with more than a quarter of a century in the direction of the St. Louis Province (as Assistant and Provincial) of the Daughters of Charity, the light of her keen intelligence and the warmth of her loving heart were an inspiration to all with whom she came in contact. Sister Catherine literally radiated love, for she lived the motto of the Daughters of Charity: "The charity of Christ urges us."

As Provincial of the St. Louis Province and successor to Sister Catherine, I feel obliged in love and justice to insure that Sister Catherine's life not lie buried in the memories of all of us who had the joy and privilege of knowing her, but rather that the light of her life and works should shine out and be an inspiration to countless other Sisters of all Communities.

As second national chairman of the Sister Formation Conference, as a member of the founding committee of Major Superiors of Women, and as co-foundress with Sister Bertrande of Marillac College for Sisters of all communities, Sister Catherine has immeasurably influenced religious life in the Church of America. It seemed fitting that this life be recorded for future generations who would meet Sister Catherine only in the pages of a book. But who could supply this figurative candlestick to enable Sister Catherine to radiate her light and warmth to posterity? Who could adequately recount the multi-faceted life of Sister Catherine and reflect the many-splendored beauty of her captivating personality?

For this labor of love, Sister Bertrande Meyers was the ideal choice. Sister Bertrande's close friendship and collaboration with Sister Catherine for over half a century enabled her to know Sister intimately. Moreover, Sister Bertrande possesses the keen insight, the delicate feeling, and the artistic skill in writing so necessary to capture in words Sister Catherine's unique and lovable personality.

In asking Sister Bertrande to write the life of Sister Catherine, I took pleasure in the thought that this book would rejoice the hearts of all of us who knew her and introduce her to countless others who will come to know and love her through this portrait. This will insure that Sister Catherine's long life of fruitful works will not lie hidden under a bushel but will shine out from the pages of this book, enkindling in all hearts the flame of her life of love.

May all who read this inspiring life feel the effects of the prayer that Sister Catherine herself chose for her death card: "May the Lord enkindle in us the flame of Charity."

SISTER MARY ROSE McPHEE

Provincial of the St. Louis Province
Daughters of Charity

ONE

"Wherever Sister Catherine was it was always spring-time," wrote her only and younger brother after attending her funeral in St. Louis on February 4, 1969. "When the sap is nourishing the trees, bringing to life their fresh green leaves, and the buds are blossoming into flowers, and the birds are singing and everywhere there is new life—that is Spring, and that was Sister Catherine during the more than seventy-five years I have known her; always Springtime."

The whole Community of Daughters of Charity felt that same sense of unconquerable joy that Sister Catherine radiated and, like an irresistible magnet, it drew Sisters and lay people alike to seek her out in time of personal sorrow or distress, knowing that they would always find an answer to their problems in the wisdom of her advice and counsel—or sometimes just in her silent, intelligent listening. "She not only has the special gift of joy," many Sisters used to remark, "but she has the even more remarkable gift of passing it on to others. It is not only what she says that comforts and cheers one in trouble, but she seems to *infuse* one's soul with joy while she speaks and listens to you." More than one Sister wrote about Sister Catherine after her death: "I know just how the disciples on the road to Emmaus felt when our Lord met them—my heart still 'burns within me' every time I recall a private interview I had with her, or on those occasions when I assisted at one of her conferences on prayer, the liturgy, or Community life."

Sister Catherine had not only the spirit of joy in abundance, but she seemed to have been given all twelve fruits of the Holy Spirit, and all seven of His gifts. But "given" is not the word, for Sister Catherine *earned*, by cooperation with grace, every virtue that became an integral part of her strong but complex character. It would be much easier to write a eulogy of Sister Catherine than to tell her life as it was down to the last moment of her eight-two years—but that would be to withhold the inspiration that comes from witnessing the growth and development of a self-made saint who used every opportunity God granted her to follow uncompromisingly, though very humanly, the rough road of the gospels which she knew was essential to any attempt at following Christ.

1

Sister Catherine was born in the then somewhat small town of Texarkana, Texas, December 9, 1886. In the Community of the Daughters of Charity, the occasion of recalling her birth date always gave rise to the lament: "Oh Sister! If only you had arrived the day before, you would have been born on the great feast of the Immaculate Conception!" In return, Sister Catherine could be counted on to dead-pan: "Oh, I really *did* arrive on the eighth, but nobody got around to noticing me until the morning of the ninth!"

She was baptized Margaret Sullivan, a fact that caused her unfeigned suffering until she was nearly nine years old. She was a remarkably precocious child, blessed with a striking quickness of mind and a loving heart. She had three older sisters, who delighted in teaching her to recite poetry, and to read fluently before she was five. All her life people expressed amazement at her remarkable vocabulary and retentive memory. While other children of her age were making superhuman efforts to read "Oh see the cow," little Margaret was reading Anderson's fairy tales. Anderson and the Brothers Grimm stimulated her already astonishingly vivid imagination to the point where she took almost as much joy in day-dreaming as she did in reading, which actually dominated her whole life.

It was that name Margaret Sullivan that started trouble. As in practically every Irish family, "Margaret" became "Maggie" overnight—and little Maggie Sullivan began to resent it as soon as she was able to read. The Sleeping Beauty wasn't named Maggie; not one of Ali Baba's Forty Thieves was called Maggie (and she insisted that girls took their rightful place among those worthies) and who would ever use "Open Maggie" as a delightful password through a magic door? But her grief went deeper than this superficial complaint: As firmly as she believed in God, Maggie believed herself to be a princess—a little princess who had been stolen by gypsies (there were many itinerant gypsies in and near the small towns of Texas) who later sold her at a great price to the Sullivans, very nice people she had to agree, but certainly not royal. If they were really noble, they would not call her Maggie.

She believed wholeheartedly that her royal family would never stop searching until they found her; and she used to sit at the gate intently watching the road for a gilded coach-and-four that would rescue the helpless little stolen princess and restore her to her rightful heritage.

It was when little Maggie Sullivan was nearing her ninth birthday that the family moved to Shreveport. Mr. Sullivan was a hotel man, and at the time owned and operated a hotel in Texarkana, Texas, and another and larger one in Shreveport. Little Maggie saw in the move an even greater possibility now of finding and being reunited forever with her royal parents, and she was certain they would reward "the Sullivans" with more golden sovereigns than they could possibly count. But the evening before they moved, she had a stern announcement to make to her family, assembled at the supper table: "We are moving to a new place," she said earnestly, "and I am *not* going to be 'Maggie Sullivan' there. Please, all of you, call me 'Madeleine'—I shall not answer to any other name."

The family was amused; but Mr. Sullivan was a scholarly and very perceptive man. He said, with great gravity of manner: "If this is Maggie's considered wish, then I ask all of you to respect that wish and call her Madeleine."

From then on the whole family called her Madeleine, and later, when nephews and nieces came along, she was always *Aunt Madeleine.*

Perceptive as Mr. Sullivan was, he could not divine her reason for the choice of the name. Could he have looked into the mind and far ranging imagination of his little daughter, he might have been distressed. The royal family from which had descended the precocious Maggie-cum-Madeleine had progressed in heraldry to a crest, to a castle, but above all to a *name.* Her royal mother was "Lady Maud Summerfield"; her father, the Duke, called his little princess, "Maudie." She chose the name Madeleine because the diminutive "Maudie" was a precious secret unto herself alone, connected only with her royal parents.

To Madeleine's lively imagination "Maudie" became daily more real. The family had hardly settled down in Shreveport when Madeleine took to going to the local post office three or four times a week.

"Is there a letter here for Maudie Summerfield?" she would ask.

Madeleine was a cute, pretty little girl who attracted attention wherever she went. The mail sorter was a rather curt no-nonsense spinster of uncertain age, but she took Madeleine's question quite seriously.

She would riffle through a stack of letters and feel sorry when she had to say, "No, there's nothing here for Maudie Summerfield—better luck next time."

But the many "next times" wore her sympathy down, so that when she saw the hopefully expectant little face of Madeleine pushing the heavy door of the post office open, she would call in exasperation from her cage, "No, little girl, there's nothing here for Maudie Summerfield."

Nothing daunted, the next morning Madeleine would slip into the post office, approach the cage, and, pushing a dime through the opening, would timidly ask for ten one-cent stamps. While her spinster friend was counting out the stamps, Madeleine would ask timidly, in a very small voice: "Is there an important letter in General Delivery for Miss Maudie Summerfield?"

11

The exasperated spinster developed a persecution complex: "Now don't ask that question again! Leave your telephone number here, and if a letter comes we'll call you. Don't you call us—we'll call you."

Frightened out of her wits at the sudden thought of what would happen at home if a letter addressed to Maudie Summerfield should arrive among the family mail, Madeleine fled and gave up visiting the post office.

2

Madeleine was registered at the Academy of the Holy Cross, in the grade school department, taught by the Daughters of the Cross. She was, at one and the same time, a cross and a crown to her long suffering teachers. Though only nine years of age, she had a stunning vocabulary, which derived from her wide reading of all sorts of books—history, biography, and above all the novels her older sisters brought home from the public library. Had she but known the grief her compulsive reading was to bring her eight or ten years later, one can surmise that she—well, quite probably, would have kept right on reading whatever the cost.

Though her head was always in a book, Madeleine was sensitive to the needs of those around her, especially her younger brother, Joe. She was kind to her older and younger sisters, Constance and Camille, but she thought Heaven could send no greater cross than to give a little boy six sisters and no brother-companion. So Madeleine became a boy in order that Joe would not become a girl. The two of them spent much time together being real boys. Of this period of their childhood, Joe writes:

My best memories of Madeleine go back to our young days when she was nine and I was going on seven. The wild things we did! I best remember that we discovered about half a mile from our home in Shreveport, beautiful little Lake Curry where there were always ten or twelve leaky boats tied up on the shore. Madeleine and I would jump into a boat, row out to where the water was deep and then we would float. Floating consisted of each one taking a turn at rowing while the other bailed out water with a big can. The challenge was to keep rowing the boat, not letting it sink while half-filled with water. It was great fun. The lake was a mile long, and about half a mile wide, infested with alligators. We could see them sunning themselves on logs and we rowed near—but not too near. We fished in this lake, too, and often we had very good luck.

Madeleine had a gift for making kites and we were both keen on flying them. I always had the best kite at school and mine, because of Madeleine's skill at making kites, flew higher than any of the other fellows.

Young as I was, I think I understood that Madeleine was trying to be a brother to me. I could count on her to cooperate in every activity I suggested, no matter how wild—and she was capable of thinking up some pretty wild ones of her own. It was my idea, I think, that since we were Texans—and inordinately proud of it—we ought to learn how to use guns. We saved up and bought two guns and a box of ammunition, and almost every afternoon we went to a vacant lot a short distance (but out of earshot) from our home and had target practice. We vied with each other in seeing who was "quickest on the draw"—that is, to put it more accurately, we counted, then shot to see whose bullet first reached the target. It was very exciting.

Another project I thought up, and Madeleine went right along with, was to go to the local hardware store and buy a pound or so of black gunpowder which we would pack in cans with a like amount of clay, put a fuse in the can, light it, and run like Indians to a safe distance. The explosion was like a war cannon going off. Needless to say, our Dad put an end to this thrilling experience.

I attended a private school near our home and Madeleine went to a nearby convent. One day she got out of school earlier than I did and she played a fine joke on me. She dressed herself in a suit of mine, put my cap on, and started to throw rocks at a brick wall which my father could see from the window of his den, where he was reading. Annoyed with the noise of rocks whizzing by and plopping against brick and wood, he opened his window and yelled to Madeleine's back: "Joe, why aren't you in school? Come in here and explain." Madeleine fled to her room and got into her own clothes. Shortly after Dad called a little louder for Joe as I turned in at our gate and went into the house. Dad looked at me thoughtfully, noticing that I had on my school suit, one entirely different than Madeleine had worn. I think that he caught on that this was just another way of Madeleine's "being a brother to me" and left it at that.

A short time after this, Madeleine and I were playing baseball. I pitched with a little too much steam, and the ball slipped through her glove, giving her a black eye any boy would be proud of. But our Dad was not impressed; he gave me the tanning of my life in spite of Madeleine's impassioned pleas for mercy.

3

In later years Sister Catherine often recalled these days with Joe, brushing aside the dangers to which they had exposed themselves. Her days were always so full of a number of things that, looking over her notes, one has to choose, select, and regretfully reject from so much source material sent from family, friends and the countless Sisters from our own Community and Sister-friends from other religious congregations.

Little Madeleine, aged about ten now, was tested at the best Catholic school in Shreveport, and placed in the sixth grade. She stood out sharply from her companions. Her wide background of reading gave her telling insights into history, biography, geography, and above all, English. She could recite from memory long passages from Tennyson's "In Memoriam," and all the characters in Idylls of the King were very real people to that famous imagination of hers. Arithmetic was her one stumbling block. She could always arrive at the right answer but from such a roundabout method that her poor teacher, standing beside her at the blackboard, could only shake her head frantically and say, "Madeleine, I just wish you could do things like other people for just once in your life! Why can't you follow the rules and solve the problem step by step?" Madeleine, always ready with a quick answer, expostulated, "But, Sister! I got the right answer, didn't I? Anyhow, I always go up steps two at a time; and when I get longer, I'll go three at a time!"

She could always turn to her best loved (eldest) sister for help. Madeleine loved this sister as wholeheartedly as she loved the nearby woods where she and Joe daily listened to the mocking birds and picked lovely flowers that kept the whole house smelling like a fragrant garden; but at this time Mamie was frankly a source of intense grief to her little sister, who hid her-

15

self in her room and cried incessantly. Mamie, the idolized "big sister," was being courted, and every day brought disaster nearer. At last the wedding day came, and little Madeleine was chief mourner as well as flower girl. When the bride and groom slipped away for their honeymoon, filling Madeleine's cup of grief to overflowing, her mother comforted, cajoled, scolded, and threatened to no avail.

Her father, an unobtrusively devout man, had long talks with her about God's Will, but little Madeleine, at that stage of life, was a far, far cry from what she was to become when religious life had molded her even then very complex personality and character. It all but broke her father's heart when he stole a look into her bedroom at night, to see the little white figure kneeling upright, praying that God would make it possible for Mamie to come home. Her mother called in the family doctor, worried about Madeleine's loss of weight. The kindly doctor, noting the too white little face, the lassitude, the loss of all that characteristic springtime buoyancy, talked to her very kindly. Her mother thought the doctor a little tactless when he patted Madeleine's head and said: "There, there, don't worry, all your other sisters will marry too, and leave home—that's just the way things are in this world." But Madeleine's reaction (as usual) was unexpected, "They can *all* move away as soon and as far as they want, if only Mamie will come home." For the first time in many days Madeleine's face brightened with hope.

The family felt relieved, but suddenly it was plunged into unexpected grief. All but Madeleine. Just six months after the wedding that had dazzled all Shreveport, Mamie was a widow, and after the funeral returned home to a sorrowing family—all but Madeleine, whose joy knew no bounds.

5

At school, the Sisters who had good reason to feel they had suffered many grievous tortures at the antic hands of Madeleine Sullivan, were happy and relieved to see that she was once again her old self—only more so. Once again she became the chattering magpie, whispering to all the girls seated next and near her. In exasperation one day, her teacher, a nervous little French-woman, stopped the class and, with dripping sarcasm, said: "Madeleine Sullivan, if what you have to say to the girls around you is of such vast importance that it cannot wait until after class, we will suspend for a few moments our study of French verbs, and listen to what you have to say." Quickly, Madeleine sprang to her feet, declaring: "Girls, unaccustomed as I am to public speaking, I feel I have something of graver importance to the world around you than the conjugation of - - -" The little French Sister actually—and excusably —*yelled* for order, and Madeleine looking aggrieved and deprived, and a little (deservedly) browbeaten, buried her head in her French grammar.

On her first fourth of July in Shreveport, Madeleine and Joe each invited four friends to bring their supply of fireworks over to their big front lawn and set the sky on fire with their wonderful sparklers, sky rockets and Roman candles. When they pooled their resources, they unanimously decided they needed a much larger supply. They took up a general collection and Madeleine was dispatched "to the city" for "more of the same."

The city was about ten minutes by trolley car from the suburb or "edge of town" where the children were gathered. Madeleine, always generous, offered to be errand-girl on one condition: they had to promise not to light a single firecracker until her return. Each placed one hand on his (or her) heart and raised the other to the sky promising

> Cross my heart and hope to die
> Before I tell a sneaky lie.

Thus, fully reassured, Madeleine boarded the summer trolley car with a full row of open windows and sailed on downtown, quickly purchasing a huge bag of assorted firecrackers, pin wheels, and so forth. On the way home, from the open windows, as the trolley edged around a hill near the Sullivan home, Madeleine could see in the now gathering dusk, her traitorous friends shooting off rainbows into the sky. Outraged at such perfidy, Madeleine quickly lit two Roman candles and, one in each hand, leaned out a window to fill the air with shooting colors. She waved them wildly at her now ashamed friends.

The wind blew the sparks back into the trolley car and the passengers screamed in panic: "Stop that, little girl, you're setting fire to all of us." But Madeleine whirled reinforcements out the open windows. Pandemonium broke loose. Finally, the poor conductor had to stop the street car. He lifted little Madeleine kindly to the platform steps, saying cheerily, "This is your stop, little girl." Madeleine reached her group, a sparkler in one hand and a Roman candle in the other, spurting blue, red and green balls into the darkening sky.

A classmate of Madeleine's, now living in St. Louis, speaking of this period in their school days, remarked:

> I remember Madeleine best as a happy-go-lucky girl. To know her was to love her. She accomplished more in her lifetime than any other person I know. As a girl she had absolutely no interest in parties or dances. She preferred baseball, climbing trees, and—unknown to her parents—playing cops and robbers with loaded pistols and her adored brother, Joe. Every day she would come running into our classroom with her dress usually torn from playing on the way to school. Each day, or each time it happened, Sister made her sit right down and mend it. Madeleine scorned sewing; she said it was a sissy's hobby. But she did as Sister told her with questionable seams, tucks, and ruffles in the most unexpected places. Madeleine suffered this for just so long, then one day appeared at the door of our classroom, a new dress ripped at the hem, and a hand sewing machine under her arm. Ever after that she used that machine for mending torn places.
>
> Madeleine's father owned a hotel in Texarkana as well as in Shreveport. One summer I went to Texarkana, Texas, for a visit. As soon as I was unpacked, I rushed over to see Madeleine. I found her in the hotel lobby, down on her knees, shining the shoes of hotel guests. Madeleine's family was well to do and the hotel could certainly afford better service than an eleven year old girl could give. "Madeleine," I cried, "Why are you always doing crazy things?" Madeleine replied loftily, "There is absolutely nothing crazy about this. The man who runs the shoe stand is home, sick in bed. He has a very large family to support, so I am taking his place so that he will not have to pay for a replacement." She added hospitably: "We can visit right here while I work."

Madeleine loved school; study and homework were

19

70- 800

no chore, since her quick mind and her ability to read with lightning speed (an ability she never lost) always allowed her time for "free reading" which became for her not many years away an almost tragic hazard; but for the present was an overwhelming delight.

6

But let us not forget the royal Summerfields. Madeleine still awaited their coming, and made suitable and dutiful preparations. Untidy to a fault, Madeleine could still wear a kimono, bathrobe, or housecoat (all of them with regal trains) with dignity. A book on her head, her head held high, she would slowly "glide" up and down the back yard to improve her carriage. After all, she had a royal goal.

This rich imagination of Madeleine's was indeed a gift, though not without its hazards, and in her adult years, adequately disciplined, was appreciated by everyone who knew her well. But at this age it took disturbing forms; for after Mamie's return Madeleine thought much about—of all things—death. This had very little to do with her brother-in-law's death, except for the possible remembrance of seeing him at first hand lying in his coffin amid flowers and overwhelming tears.

But again, so unlike the later woman the Community molded into a strong, outgoing, joyous Daughter of Charity, little Madeleine "enjoyed" her own tree house, where no one ever dared intrude on her special half-hour visit each day. There she reflected deeply on the superficial aspects of death. Down to the last detail she planned her own funeral—a lavishly beautiful white casket, bedecked with the kind of wild flowers she and Joe picked in the woods, faithfully continuing to keep the house supplied. She selected the girls she liked best in class for her pallbearers. The rest of her classmates preceded the funeral cortege, scattering flower petals as they walked with measured step to the church. And lo! arrived at last, but alas too late, there at the vestibule of the church stood Lord and Lady Summerfield weeping wildly, while the organ played, a little reproachfully, "Too late, Too late." (Madeleine had recently been one of the foolish virgins in a Biblical play at school—meriting the part for nearly always being late for school.)

At this overwhelming moment in The Death of Maudie Summerfield, Madeleine would burst into tears, weeping for the whole world because everyone in it would some day die. This make-believe was Madeleine's favorite pastime, outside of reading; but often, allured by books, she would climb down from her tree house still sobbing out loud. She kept the tree houses's purpose and the funeral she so much "enjoyed" a dead secret, until one day her beloved Mamie discovered her at the foot of the tree, sobbing her heart out with very real tears streaming down her cheeks. Unable to get any sensible explanation from little Madeleine, she brought her to her mother. Mrs. Sullivan, "the sunniest woman in Shreveport" with a heart as big as her house, simply remarked: "Don't be prying into the child's business," and (always ready to spoil each of her seven children) put little Madeleine to bed, bathed her hot forehead, sat by her until she had consumed some cookies and milk, then advised her little daughter to "take a nice long nap—and you can have a tray for supper!" As soon as the door closed on her mother, Madeleine reached happily under her pillow for *Beverly of Grau-stark*, the book she was reading at the time, revelling in the fact that she could read all afternoon and evening in bed without having to help with the suppertime dishes!

7

Madeleine breezed through high school in three years, carrying straight A's on her report card, and ending up with the leading part in the class play, and valedictorian of her class—six months before her sixteenth birthday. Though remarkably mature for her age, her love of fun drove her teachers wild, it was expressed in such extraordinary ways. She delighted in serving her elder sisters in their search after the goddess beauty, which at that time was concerned with hair styling and beguiling do-it-yourself advertisements assuring the "young woman who really cares can learn to synchronize good grooming with proper hair color."

Mamie, Sue, and Elizabeth (her closest in age) vied with one another in securing the patient services of Madeleine in "modeling" a hair dye until just the most perfect choice could be made. Thus it was that Mamie (who was again being "courted") would dunk Madeleine's head in a bubbly concoction of amber liquid, which, when withdrawn and thoroughly dried, turned Madeleine into an overnight blonde. When, with her own hand and the aid of modern hair irons (circa 1900), Mamie deftly twisted the golden hair into a halo of tiny, very tight curls all over her head, Madeleine stepped forth a home-made but irresistible blue-eyed cherub. When Madeleine appeared in the classroom on Monday morning (with the hand sewing machine under her arm, for hems still somehow got caught on picket fences), the girls gaped open-mouthed at her crowning glory, her once mousey-brown tendrils now flawlessly gold. Her teachers remained speechless for the first hour of class; but the students loved and imitated it, often with hilarious effect.

The following Monday, Sue's effort had turned Madeleine into a very coal black brunette, with ringlets tossing about her shoulders. On this occasion her Sister-teacher ventured to tell her crossly that her hair "looked cheap." "Why Sister," Madeleine looking up so that Sister would get the full force of her slanted oriental eyes and blackened eyebrows (which were naturally thick) "my sister Sue spent over nine dollars beautifying me this way." The next Monday, under Elizabeth's flaming artistry, Madeleine arrived a flashing redhead in a green dress—torn at the hem.

8

The Sullivan pew was fourth from the altar; parishioners found it a moving sight each Sunday to see Mr. Sullivan, shepherding into Church his brood of seven, each supplied with a prayer book, according to age: the little ones with "A Child's Prayer Book," the middle ones with "Devotions" with fascinating color illustrations; Madeleine, Mamie, Sue and her father carried "The Key to Heaven." Of course, among the three youngest, Joe, Constance and Camille, there was much swapping of texts during the sermon.

It was at the beginning of her freshman year that Madeleine began to think seriously about her future.

The daily examples of her teachers—her ever beloved Daughters of the Cross—their patience (which now and then Madeleine disturbed mightily) and cordiality with all "their girls" impressed Madeleine deeply. Here in the convent was a life of purpose, of zeal to mold Catholic women of the future, and this goal was not lost on Madeleine. There was one nun, Sister Loretto, that Madeleine had a special fondness for and she decided to open her heart to her. But oddly enough she could never bring herself to speak of a religious vocation. Finally, she realized that she was entering her senior year, and she simply must consult Sister Loretto about her vocation. But she, who could readily and eagerly talk like a Philadelphia lawyer at any time and any place, found her tongue tied when it came to this subject.

Then one day she thought up the perfect plan. She would ask her mother (who knew nothing of her religious aspirations) if she could take *private* lessons in public speaking under Sister Loretto, head of the speech department at school. Her mother readily agreed and told Madeleine to make her own financial arrangements, which Madeleine did with great alacrity. Sister Loretto was delighted for two good reasons; she wholeheartedly liked Madeleine Sullivan, but she also recognized her unusual ability in the theatrical field. Here would be a chance to pump life into the speech and drama department. And here, thought Madeleine, was her own main chance. Now she would talk over entering the Community of Daughters of the Cross.

Lessons with Sister Loretto were three times a week, and each time that Madeleine entered the classroom she would vow to herself: "Now, today, this minute I'll tell her." But the words froze on her lips, so that

Madeleine graduated from the Holy Cross Academy (A Select School for Young Ladies) without ever making open declaration of her lofty design.

9

The summer passed, and Madeleine, still only fifteen years of age, entered a business college to learn speed typewriting. This made small demand on her intellectual powers and especially on her time, so she had more and more leisure for reading. About this time Gobillon's *Life of St. Vincent* and Lady Lovat's *Life of St. Louise de Marillac* fell into her hands. (Her father had a remarkable library of biography, which was Madeleine's favorite form of reading.) She devoured the chapters in each book that told of the founding of the Community of Daughters of Charity with their exciting works. In imagination, Madeleine saw herself variously as a Daughter of Charity, teaching little children to know and love God while learning the three R's; she saw herself a mother to orphans, and a friend to all men, whatever their need. Like a Biblical miracle of restoring the deaf to hearing and the dumb to speech, Madeleine no longer stuttered and stammered when the conversation turned to religious vocations, but was quite vocal now about becoming a Daughter of Charity.

Around January 11 or 12, the Sullivans had a visitor. Mrs. Sullivan was almost a connoisseur of priests; she loved to have them come for lunch or dinner and the whole family enjoyed these visits. This time, by some coincidence, it was a Father Sullivan, S.J., (no relation) who stopped over in Shreveport between trains en route to Dallas, Texas. Madeleine (always articulate) turned the subject to her own interests.

"Father," she said, "do you know any Daughters of Charity? I know New Orleans is full of them, but I've never seen one."

Madeleine had let down the net and it came up loaded to the breaking point. Father was in his glory, telling the glowing history of the Community in Louisiana and throughout the United States. "I'll be staying at their hospital in Dallas tonight," he said, and added playfully, "Want to come along and meet the Daughters?"

Madeleine sprang up from the table, ready to pack at once.

"Tut, tut," Father Sullivan said, "my train doesn't leave before six. There are a few things you ought to know about the Daughters," and, obviously ill-informed but believing it to be the truth, he said: "You have to be a registered nurse before you can enter that Order. Haven't I told you about their service to wounded soldiers in the Civil War—Angels of the Battlefield, they called them?"

"I'd love any battlefield, Father, but I'd really hate nursing," said Madeleine, afraid she was facing a dying dream.

"What difference does it make what you do?" asked Father Sullivan. "Isn't dedicating yourself to a self-sacrificing love of God the important thing? Isn't *that* what a religious vocation is all about?"

Madeleine thought that over for a few minutes, then said briskly: "I'll be at the station before six o'clock!"

TWO

Father Sullivan, S.J. and Madeleine Sullivan arrived in Dallas late that night. The Sister delegated to wait up for Father Sullivan was agreeably surprised when he introduced a tall, willowy, good-looking girl as an applicant for the school of nursing. By tacit agreement with Father, Madeleine said nothing of her desire to enter the Community, but was received as a "probationer" simplified to "probie" as was the custom in schools of nursing at the time. In those days student and graduate nurses alike worked unreasonably hard, not only in nursing the sick, but in doing the household chores of aides, maids, and nurse all in one.

Madeleine threw herself wholeheartedly into her new profession. She was by nature a poor, untidy housekeeper (having seldom lifted a hand to any kind of housework at home) and she exhibited neither affinity nor efficiency in nursing. But she was so unconquerably cheery, compassionate and kind to her patients that she daily became more and more the most popular nurse on any hall to which she was assigned. She was a fascinating conversationalist and kept her patients entertained with good book discussions, reading them excerpts from the morning newspapers, or passages from well chosen short stories. What if there was a little Texas dust on the tables and window sills? Nobody complained about Miss Sullivan as a nurse.

Madeleine would have made a wonderful doctor of medicine; she loved the book work pertaining to the profession; and she was a born teacher. She could lecture on anatomy and physiology with blackboard illustrations, showing skeptical Texan students how the various systems of the body work so that the most hardheaded, boasting, self-styled atheists among them were confounded when asked to explain how anyone but God could create man—or a flea, for that matter.

1

Among the Sisters with whom Madeleine worked at this time, there was one, Sister Ursula Fenton, who took a very particular interest in the young nurse-to-be. She thought that Madeleine was overworking to a dangerous degree; but Madeleine would always insist that work was fun and besides, with an acute shortage of personnel in every department, what was there to do! But Sister Ursula proved to be only too right, and in Madeleine's second year of study Sister Ursula insisted that she have a complete check-up. The doctor's verdict was that they had "isolated just in time" a bug that spelt incipient tuberculosis. He advised that she take a year's leave of absence, spending as much time as possible in the open air, doing absolutely nothing but camping, fishing, reading and sleeping.

Madeleine realized that what she needed more than anything else was rest; she felt close to exhaustion, so she took a year's leave of absence. During the year and a half or so that she had been in Dallas, the family had moved back to Texarkana and there Madeleine went to talk things over with her mother. "Sure and we'll have ye well in no time," her cheerful mother said, looking her over shrewdly. "It's some good old homemade cooking you're after needing. After ye've put a few pounds on your bones, you and Elizabeth can get sleeping bags and camping equipment and start down the Texas trails wherever they lead." The two girls adored the prospect of living in trees and fishing in streams, but, for Madeleine, reading undisturbed was her joy forever.

When, after the greater part of a year as Texas vagabonds, the girls returned to Texarkana, Mr. and Mrs. Sullivan's joy knew no bounds at seeing Madeleine perfectly well—cheeks rounded out like cherries, and the old joyous twinkle back again in her really startlingly blue eyes. And she simply could not wait to get back to Dallas—and Sister Ursula Fenton.

Once again back in Dallas, Sister Ursula met her with the news that she had been missioned to Providence Hospital in Waco, Texas, where she was to found and organize a school of nursing. At that time, Waco was a very Protestant town (it still is) and starting a school of nursing would be a difficult task. Sister Ursula asked Madeleine (Miss Sullivan as she was professionally called) to come to Waco with her and finish her training there. In a spirit of "Whither thou goest, I go too" Madeleine was pleased and happy to pioneer in the school of nursing. She was the only student, for the first semester, but somehow more girls were attracted to the school and in another year they had a satisfactory number of probies. Again, Madeleine was the highest ranking student—in a class of one.

2

In Waco, Madeleine met two Sisters who were to figure significantly in her life. One was the Sister-Servant, which is the title the Daughters of Charity have given the local superior during its more than three hundred-thirty years of existence. Sister Gabriel Murtagh was something of a rigorist, a person with strong views, but rather narrow in her outlook on persons, places and things. She took a dim view of Madeleine's colorful personality. The other person of importance to Madeleine was Sister Stella Lacey on whose hall she served.

Sister Stella loved fun, and Madeleine was right there to supply it. She worked under Sister Stella's guidance, and her generosity became a legend, passed on to students in their first year of training.

Sister Gabriel Murtagh felt that Madeleine was forming too strong an attachment to Sister Stella so she sent for her one day to go into the matter. Her opening gambit was: "Miss Sullivan, you love Sister Stella very much, don't you?"

"Oh my yes," answered Madeleine, her face lighting up with smiles, "and I love Sister Ursula, too—why Sister, I love just about everybody!"

Sister Gabriel was quiet for a moment. "But I think," she said, "you are *attached* to Sister Stella." In Madeleine's vivid imagination she saw herself in kaleidoscopic pictures: A horse *attached* to a buggy; an electric light *attached* to a switch, a kite *attached* to a string, and herself *attached* to Sister Stella. She did not want to laugh, but her unusually deep dimples in both cheeks gave her away.

Sister Gabriel took a sterner attitude: "Stop laughing," she ordered. "You can never be serious for ten minutes at a time."

It was the worst possible moment for Madeleine to

come out with what she did but, for weal or woe, her face was no longer smiling. "Oh Sister, I can be very serious when the situation calls for it. In fact, right now I'd like to talk to you about something very serious. Sister, I want to be a Daughter of Charity as soon as I graduate."

Sister Gabriel closed her eyes and turned very white. Madeleine, believing that Sister Gabriel was in a state of shock, tip-toed from the room. "At last," she said to herself, "I got it out into the open; I've told her, and now I can really begin to plan my future."

But the direct result of the interview was that Miss Sullivan was changed from Sister Stella's hall and replaced by someone less susceptible—and certainly less fun. In changing her place of duty, Sister Gabriel told Madeleine: "Now remember this—I forbid you to put your foot on Sister Stella's floor."

A short time later, Sister Stella was in the diet kitchen. (In those days, more than sixty years ago, there was one on each floor from which meals could be prepared and served.) Sister Stella, preoccupied and worried, suddenly heard a bumping and a banging, and a pushing. She stood dead still in her tracks as she faced the dumb-waiter, watching the door slowly, and with difficulty, pushed back. Lo, there with her nearly six feet of lankiness, wrapped like a ball of twine, was— Madeleine. Sister Stella could not refrain from laughing as Madeleine partially straightened up so she could explain. Sister Stella, however, spoke first: "Miss Sullivan," she said sternly, "you told me that you had been forbidden to put your foot on this floor! I cannot go along with your disobedience."

Madeleine was crushed. Where she had expected

cordiality and praise, she received coldness and no appreciation at all for her ingenuity. "Why, Sister," she said ruefully, "how can you say such things? I am not going to put a foot on your floor—not once; but I simply do have to *see* you from time to time. I need your counsel, and that's one of the gifts of the Holy Ghost, given to *you* by Him for *me*."

Then she told Sister Stella about announcing her intention of becoming a Daughter. Sister Stella burst out laughing: "You could have chosen a better psychological moment for your big news, couldn't you?"

"No, I couldn't, Sister. Back in high school I wanted to say something about my vocation, but I could never get the words out. I think I was truly inspired. Now I have spoken."

But her only answer to the great tidings was a thudding silence from Sister Gabriel. A month or so later, Madeleine sought her out again: "Sister, could we talk about my becoming a Daughter of Charity?"

Sister Gabriel could only look at her blankly: "Miss Sullivan," she said slowly and deliberately, "what on earth makes you think you could be a Sister—do you really think you have a religious vocation?"

Just as slowly and just as deliberately, Madeleine answered: "Well, I really didn't think so at first when I was ten. And it honestly wasn't my idea in the beginning. It was actually God's inspiration and I went right along with Him."

The room was very still for awhile, then Sister Gabriel spoke: "I will never put in your application," she said finally; "I don't think you have a vocation."

Madeleine rose with cheerful dignity. "Thank you, Sister, for being honest with me; I shall be back in a month to see if you have changed your mind; and, if not, then let us explore *why* not."

Madeleine chose a Sunday, a month later, for the interview. She opened the discussion with a question: "Sister Gabriel, just *why* are you so unwilling to send in my application to enter the Community?"

Sister Gabriel was evasive, speaking vaguely of difficulties and trials allotted to those who dedicate themselves to God to live as He did when He came in human form to be our way, our truth, and our life.

Madeleine listened, weighing each word intelligently, and then defended herself. "Don't you think I could, with spiritual guidance, learn to be a good religious?" When there was no answer to this question, Madeleine was almost angry. "Sister," she said, her voice trembling, "you have something specific in mind about me and I want to know what it is."

Then the skies opened and one accusing sentence fell on her ears like thunder. Sister Gabriel said: "You read too much."

Madeleine looked aghast at her. "Is reading a bad thing?" she asked rather faintly.

"Well, of course," Sister said in a kinder tone, "the lives of the saints, some helpful spiritual writers—but what do you read?" she asked in harsher tones. "You read *The Life of Napoleon* (how can his example help you?); you read those silly Ouida books (all the rage in the 1900's); and (raising her eyes to Heaven) you read flamboyant *love* stories."

Madeleine was honestly bewildered. "Sister Gabriel," she said earnestly, "if one plans to reject the world with all its foolishness, don't you think it is wise to know, even vicariously, what one is rejecting?"

Sister Gabriel had no time for philosophizing. "You asked me *why* I won't put in your application, and I've told you," she said with a sigh of relief that this preposterous question was settled forever.

But she underestimated Madeleine's persistence. After long moments of silence between them, Madeleine spoke: "Sister, they used to say at home that I seemed to need reading the way other people need air and food and drink. But it's a small sacrifice to make for our Lord. If I promise you that I will not read so much as a newspaper for one whole year, will you apply for me then?"

Sister Gabriel, who believed that Miss Sullivan could not last a week without breaking down and reading, eyed her with a sparkle in her eye. "Yes," she said, more touched at Madeleine's earnestness than she would permit herself to show; "yes, if you'll promise me that you will not open a book (except your textbooks), I will write your application at the end of a full year."

Madeleine promised joyfully, asking warily, however, "Is this a promise from you, too?" Sister Gabriel promised quite solemnly, feeling quite sure she would never have to write that application.

Madeleine looked carefully at the clock, then gave a calendar careful scrutiny, writing in her notebook the portentous year, month, and date of these fateful proceedings. Handing a copy of her written memo as to dates and days to Sister Gabriel and later to Sister Ursula, Sister Stella, and several of the nurses with whom she worked, and especially her room-mate, Madeleine made a public pledge of no more reading for a year, which promise she most scrupulously kept to the letter. No one but God and herself knew what a pearl of great price this was that she offered at the feet of her King; but it must be written in gold in the book of life.

One year to the very day of the "bargain"—the solemn promises—Madeleine appeared at the office door where Sister Gabriel was sorting mail. With a radiant face and smiling lips, she said: "Sister Gabriel, I have been true to my promise. May I put in my application today?"

To Madeleine's sincere horror, Sister Gabriel welshed. "It is a very commendable sacrifice you have made, Miss Sullivan, but I cannot reconcile my conscience to the promise I made—and it sometimes takes great courage to break a promise that should not have been made in the first place . . . My conscience . . ."

Her voice trailed away, but Madeleine barely restrained her anger, as she replied firmly: "Sister, I am appalled. A promise made in good faith is something to be kept. It took great courage for me to make that promise, and more, to keep it. But now I am released from it." She left the office.

Late that evening, Sister Gabriel knocked at the door of Madeleine's room. She found—to her horror—Madeleine thrown across the bed, lying on her stomach, reading like a house afire *The Cricket on the Hearth*. "AHA," Sister Gabriel cried, pointing an accusing finger, "you're READING!" as if Madeleine might have been safe-breaking . . . Who knows? At that very moment Sister Gabriel might have had a change of heart.

But Madeleine rose to acknowledge Sister's presence, and to her accusation replied very quietly: "Yes, Sister, I began to read exactly five minutes after you broke your promise."

The next morning, in the diet kitchen, Sister Stella, kind, faithful Sister Stella, heard the well-known bumping, creaking, banging dumb-waiter on the ascent to her diet kitchen. The door opened, and Madeleine, curled up like a snail, careful to keep both feet off "that floor," tearfully shared the sad news that she was no nearer her goal than she was four years ago. "Tell me how you really feel about this, Miss Sullivan—deep down inside. Are you discouraged?"

Madeleine's calm blue eyes met Sister Stella's and dried instantly. "Deep down, Sister, I feel a quiet, untouchable peace. I know this is what God wants for me at this moment; but this moment won't stand still forever. I shall and I will become a Daughter of Charity," and she added wistfully, "maybe we'll live together some day. If we do, you'll feel rewarded for all the prayers you have said and are saying for me." And with a cheery wave—as cheerily as she could manage in her restricted quarters, she descended to floors where her "feet" could touch without peril.

"Maybe we'll live together," Madeleine had said . . . How different the gay prophecy from the stark reality of its future fulfillment.

4

Madeleine was graduated in 1908, the first and only graduate in the fledgling School of Nursing, in Waco, Texas. Sister Ursula was pleased as punch; more students had enrolled, and Madeleine had been like a "big sister" to them. Now, what with the six month's probation, the year and a half out for illness, it had taken five years to reach this special day. She went home for a visit with the family. Home once more meant Texarkana, Texas, where the family moved again in 1903. She rested, rode horses, and managed to read a book a day.

One day, most unexpectedly, Madeleine received a letter from Sister Ursula, asking her to come lend a hand, as the hospital was very busy and she needed a graduate to supervise one of the busiest halls. With great joy, Madeleine managed to get off the same day. Sister Ursula told her almost immediately that she wanted her to meet a priest visitor. That was a momentous day in the life and annals of Madeleine Sullivan.

"This is Father Sullivan, a Vincentian priest, and— hold your breath; he is the Reverend Director of the Daughters of Charity." Madeleine looked at the elderly priest, the white hair, so thick and white it looked like a chrysanthemum, and beneath the hair she saw the kindest face she had ever looked at in her whole life.

Sister Ursula quietly withdrew from the parlor and that day began a long and wonderful friendship which lasted nineteen years, that is until Father Sullivan died in 1927. Madeleine opened her whole heart to him about her vocation, and his eyes shone with deep sympathy. Father Sullivan stayed three days at Waco, and Madeleine managed to meet him each day for serious talks.

On the last day of his visit, Madeleine slipped into the dining room to say goodby. By chance, but more truly by divine Providence, Sister Gabriel came into the room without seeing Madeleine, who rose in her rather casual way and said: "Sister, the Sullivans meet again."

Father beamed at her, saying to Sister Gabriel: "Sister, we need more Sullivans in the Community—and we need them right away—how nice if the new province opens with a 'Sister Sullivan' in the Seminary (the Daughter of Charity's term for novitiate). Now wouldn't that please me! You see, I have five nieces in the Congregation of St. Joseph, but not one among the Daughters! We must correct that, and soon."

The next morning Madeleine placed her application for entrance into the Community of Daughters of Charity; a week later she received word from St. Louis that she had been accepted and named to postulate at St. Paul's Hospital in Dallas, Texas.

THREE

On January 11, 1909, Madeleine became a postulant at St. Paul's in Dallas, Texas, and as such was called Miss Sullivan. The Sister Servant of St. Paul's Sanitarium (later the name was changed to St. Paul Hospital) was Sister Camilla Broden, remembered even today as a "perfect lady" in her grooming, manner of speaking, and kindness. She was delighted to welcome Miss Sullivan as a postulant, as well as a graduate nurse, who would be very useful as supervisor of a hall. But most of all she rejoiced to see that Miss Sullivan was no neophyte in the spiritual life. She radiated, in an unostentatious way, the joyousness of the interior life without any pious postures.

She brought to the Community a kind heart, a love for all the Sisters, and for all with whom she worked, and she made laughter a common event wherever she was with her perceptive wit, a natural gaiety, and a ready repartee. But never was her wit spiced with satire or sarcasm, or anything that could in any way hurt those with whom she exchanged conversation. Miss Sullivan had brought the *sui generis* Madeleine with her into postulatum—the first steps in the religious life, and wherever Madeleine was, not only was it always springtime, but something always happened.

1

Madeleine knew Dallas as well as Waco, having spent about a year and a half as a student nurse there.

She was thus able to go on errands for Sister Camilla, from time to time; and Madeleine, who had by no means "shed the world" as yet, often took a little extra time to go window-shopping, mingling with the crowds with no tinge of self-consciousness.

Madeleine contributed generously to the evening recreation with the Sisters, exchanging funny anecdotes of things that happened to her, telling it in her inimitable way that always provoked spontaneous laughter. On the evening of a day that she had gone downtown on errands for Sister Camilla, she came to recreation bursting to tell of the day's unusual happening. When a lull in conversation gave Miss Sullivan her chance, she cried out gaily: "Oh Sisters! Guess what happened to *me today!* You'll never guess in a thousand years! The Sisters who knew whatever had happened was good for a laugh said: "Since we can't guess in a thousand years, why not tell us *now?*" Madeleine was only too ready. Without warning she raised her voice and in a dramatic manner announced: "I have this day been to a Fortune Teller, Madame Celeste Divine, who knows all and tells all for twenty-five cents."

It was like a bomb striking the Community Room table, around which the Sisters sat sewing. One senior Sister dropped what she was doing, crossed herself and said in a quavering voice: "A fortune teller! Why, Miss Sullivan, that's a sin." Sister Camilla, somewhat pale and slightly unnerved, spoke in her always gentle and pleasant voice: "What an experience, Miss Sullivan! Is it a secret what the divine Celeste told you?"

Madeleine knew there was something wrong here—and quite possibly expected a different response. "Oh, do let me tell you everything," she rushed on, a trifle nervous now. "It was hilarious. Madame was seated in her salon, several gilded ice-cream-parlor chairs giving a touch of elegance to the wall-draped room. She occupied a chair on a red velvet dais, a small table before her and another and smaller chair for the client, whom she referred to as *The Seeker after Truth*. She was draped in a large paisley shawl fringed with little golden balls. On her black cascading hair she wore a yellow silk mantillo. In a deep, throaty voice she said, extending a hand across the table to me: "Cross my palm with a silver coin." I put a quarter in the center of her palm and waited—a tiny bit scared, it all looked so gruesome. She looked me over carefully, from my black hat, black blouse, black skirt, to my black hose and shoes, and, in sepulchral tones, said shrewdly: "You are bereaved now, but a silver cloud is on the horizon. He will come, my friend, he will come!"

"Oh, He's here," I said airily. "I've given Him my hand and my heart forever."

"Celeste caught herself quickly, as though I had anticipated her message from the spirit world and cleverly managed not to show any surprise that, with all this happy anticipation, I still sported widow's weeds."

"Ah, I knew it would be so. Therefore, I can give you glad tidings. This person will soon propose a long, long journey. Take it without fear, lady, a whole new life will open up before you as you cross the horizon where the rainbow ends."

"Oh," I said, breathless with joy, and, at the same time, afraid of my life that I would get home late for meditation. "Thank you." I withdrew from the commanding presence of Madame Celeste Divine and got on the nearest streetcar for home.

Miss Sullivan's recital was punctuated with many spontaneous bursts of laughter from her enraptured audience as she concluded her adventure. But the next morning she found at her place in the Community Room a small pamphlet, a reprint of an article on "The Church's Attitude towards Spiritualism, Seances and Fortune Telling." It contained a card with a brief but pleasant message from Sister Camilla: "Thank you for a spirited recreation last night. We appreciate our Miss Sullivan." Madeleine got the message.

2

Less than a week later, and again at recreation, one of the Sisters remarked brightly: "Oh, I dreamed of Madame Celeste Divine last night!" There was a whoop of laughter. No one had mentioned her since Miss Sullivan's account of her visit to her salon. Sister Camilla tinkled her little bell, which signified an announcement. "Can it be that the divine Celeste walks again?" she asked with a smile at Miss Sullivan. She pulled a telegram from her pocket. "Just listen to this!" She read:

> Arriving tomorrow morning, February 18, T & P Railroad.
>
>> Father James J. Sullivan, C.M.

Madeleine clapped her hands excitedly, "Maybe he'll propose a long journey," she said laughingly. "Over the rainbow," added another Sister. Still another said: "St. Louis may be 'over the rainbow' but you're not here quite six weeks yet, honey. You have seven weeks more to go." While yet another predicted *sotto voce,* "and back to Texarkana, if you intend visiting any more fortune tellers." Madeleine took their teasing in good part and, impersonating the stentorian tones of Madame Celeste, said: "We shall see what we shall see."

What they saw was this:

Madeleine slipped into the dining room where Father Sullivan was having breakfast. She told him of her foolish visit to Madame Celeste, adding, "I did it just for fun, Father, on the spur of the moment. I really know better. . ." Madeleine noted the fleeting look of unease that clouded Father Sullivan's face. But all he said was, "I shouldn't have done that, my child; however, people who never make mistakes never really learn to live. . ." There was a brief silence, Madeleine's blue eyes eloquently contrite. Then Father Sullivan chuckled. "Don't be worried. How would you like *me* to tell your fortune?" Madeleine smiled as though a great stone had been lifted from her heart. "Well," said Father Sullivan, an impish twinkle in his eye, "I propose you take a long journey." Madeleine held her breath. "Tomorrow is George Washington's birthday. My business is concluded here. If you can be ready by tomorrow for the noon T&P, you'll be in time for the Seminary entrance retreat which opens the morning of February 23 and lasts for three days. When you come out of that retreat, you will be a member of the Community and, for the duration of your Seminary, you will be called Sister Sullivan."

"But Father! I have been postulating only six weeks! Do you think I'm ready?" Father Sullivan chuckled again. "Don't you think you did a little postulating at

Waco? Maybe this will make up for that year of abstention from reading. What do you think?"

"Well," Madeleine replied, her lips trembling a little, "the thought is not very original, but I think God is simply wonderful!"

3

The travelers arrived early in St. Louis and Miss Sullivan was just in time for her entrance three-day retreat. The province was newly divided into an "Eastern Province," with headquarters at Emmitsburg, and a "Western Province," with temporary headquarters located on the top floor of St. Vincent's Institution (a hospital for the mentally ill) while awaiting the construction of a new provincial house in Normandy, a suburb of St. Louis.

In order to organize a Seminary (novitiate) as soon as possible, Emmitsburg loaned for one year Sister Augustine Park, the long-time Directress of their Seminary. Sister Augustine was one of the great women in the annals of the Community. With her she brought three Seminary Sisters (novices) who had spent some time under her guidance, and would know how to help the newcomers to adjust to the strange new world-within-a-world that was the Seminary in 1909. The Seminary Sisters from the east were originally from states within the new Western province, so they were happy to be nearer home. Making the retreat with Sister Sullivan were Sister Zoe Donnelly and Sister Elizabeth Lewis—they became "Sisters" on February 26 and, throughout their entire Community life, "kept in touch."

Sister Sullivan took to the Seminary as the thirsty stag to a mountain stream. She reveled in the atmosphere of silence and solitude. She was the life of recreation with her fund of amusing anecdotes, her willingness to recite the more dramatic poetry (?) of the repertoire that she learned in her "elocution lessons" with Sister Loretto, Daughter of the Cross. Reminiscent of Madeleine, as we saw her in her Shreveport days, is her Seminary Record:

> *Margaret Sullivan.* Almost twenty-three years of age, born in Texarkana, Texas. Tall, healthy, good, very kind to her companions, obedient, unaffected, very generous in the practice of humility. Knows little of domestic duties but most willing to learn, a great talker, excellent in English, a graduate nurse, untidy.

4

Madeleine, with her companions, received the Holy Habit on November 26, 1909, and was given the name Sister Catherine. A few days later, she left for her first assignment, St. Thomas Hospital, Nashville, Tennessee. She was greeted with great warmth by the Sisters and felt a "sense of belonging" due in great part to Sister Scholastica Kehoe, her first Sister Servant. It is an amusing fact that Sister Catherine could have spent a year in the hands of Sister Augustine Park, "a perfect lady," (the word 'perfect lady' implies in this context— along with other such traits as gentleness, soft-spokenness—an unaffected but marked fastidiousness both as regards manner of speech and grooming) and was now to spend another year with another "perfect lady," in the sense described, and still be evaluated by both as "untidy". . . . The probable cause lay in the fact that Sister Catherine was so attractive, so outgoing, so lovable that each superior thought she ought to be allowed at least one fault among the many solid virtues that were so manifest in her strong character. Sister Catherine was in no hurry to correct her untidiness, believing that too-careful grooming was the mark of a small mind. But she was to correct that fault one day in the future in a way that gives striking insights into how Sister Catherine became a self-made saint. Meantime she remained untidy until God's good time.

5

Sister Catherine was happy and contented in her work at St. Thomas Hospital, although she could never bring herself to anything more than a very supernatural liking for nursing itself. She loved people, however— patients, colleagues, the hospital personnel, and she was very happy in her work. As supervisor of a hall one of her responsibilities was to teach the students to keep clear, concise and correct charts, so that doctors and relief-nurses would better understand the patients' needs. Sister Catherine went over these charts herself and was tact itself in pointing out where the young students could use a more explicit phrase, or a more apt word to describe a patient's condition. To her great amusement one morning, she found a young nurse had recorded of her special patient: "Kidneys moved." Sister Catherine wrote in red ink: "Where to?"

The nurses loved Sister Catherine because she was essentially lovable, kind and understanding. Several of them kept up a lifelong correspondence with her. One can imagine their grief one morning when, assembled at the nurses' station to give and hear reports from night and early morning shifts, Sister Catherine told "her girls" that Sister Scholastica had just received a telegram to send Sister Catherine to St. Louis, and that she would be replaced by another Sister in a short time. Although the "girls" (many of them graduate nurses who had served at St. Thomas Hospital for more than a decade) wept, Sister Catherine smiled and remarked: "Life is ahead of you, girls. Learn to live it a day at a time; otherwise life gets to be a bit of a much-too-much sort of thing and we lose perspective." She had occasion to recall these words in the nearby future; words which are more easily preached than practiced by frail human nature.

Fortified with two years of mission experience, Sister Catherine returned to St. Louis to find herself assigned to the office of third Directress of the Seminary. After one year spent in organizing and forming the Seminary Sisters (novices) of the western province, Sister Augustine Park returned to Emmitsburg and resumed her duties as Directress of the Seminary there. Sister Augustine was replaced by Sister Baptista Lynch.

6

Sister Augustine Park was born to be a Seminary Directress. She was a model Daughter of Charity, kind but very firm, an inspiring leader—one who formed soldiers as well as Sisters who, in her opinion, through sustained effort could well become saints. She sought to insert steel into the backbone of each Seminary Sister, and the transformations she achieved with God's grace placed the newly formed western province forever in her debt. Sister Catherine had admired and loved her dearly as her Directress and clung tenaciously to the ideals and principles she had so forcefully inculcated.

The second Directress, Sister Madeleine Morris, was a Sister from Emmitsburg who had been sent to be the strong right arm of Sister Baptista and, at the same time, an understudy to replace her as first Directress within a year or two. Sister Madeleine (another perfect lady) held the same ideals and principles as Sister Augustine Park and the same ideas about the "how" of formation of a religious character and personality. It was her contention that, just as the sacrament of Baptism conferred sanctifying grace on these candidates for the religious life, so the sacrament of Confirmation made them potential soldiers of Jesus Christ and (potential) heirs of the kingdom of Heaven.

Sister Madeleine contended that soldiers needed self-control, discipline, courage and strength of character. She believed that these goals could not be nourished by the milk of human kindness alone, nor would these goals be achieved by unlimited permissiveness. She was, consequently, impatient with what she called the "grand-motherliness" of Sister Baptista, not stopping to think that to be over-indulgent was basic to Sister Baptista's character, which could not be changed at her age. Nor, to be fair, had Sister Baptista asked for this assignment which was really made to order for Sister Madeleine, but not for Sister Baptista herself.

Sister Catherine grew to love Sister Madeleine deeply. She matched Sister Catherine in wit, intellect, and love of fun, and out of this year together bloomed a lifetime friendship. Sister Catherine was of the same mind about character formation as were Sister Augus-

48

tine and Sister Madeleine, but she made desperate efforts to modify the method of attaining these ideals for the sake of peace. Sister Madeleine could not, or would not, compromise. Sister Catherine was capable of bearing many burdens, but disharmony was not one of them. With her shrewd insight, she knew that disharmony is, by its nature, disruptive and no matter how prudently one tries to hide its existence, young eyes see more clearly and are far less mellow in their judgments of human nature than are the more experienced.

It was part of Sister Catherine's life-style never to speak and never to listen to uncharitable remarks about others. In the presence of fault finding or any kind of unconstructive criticism, her silence was like a lowering two-edged sword. Caught as she was in this conflict of personalities, she wore herself out praying and doing penance, consoled by one happy factor: the evening recreation was always hilarious and healing. For Sister Madeleine, with an active ally in Sister Catherine, could so vary each night's period of relaxation that all participated and, in sharing themselves under the unobtrusive leadership of Sister Madeleine, laughter made it possible for the day's frictions, frustrations and conflicts to disappear.

But they reared their ugly heads at dawn and persisted through the day: A permission granted out of an over-indulgent kindness by the first Directress; the same permission greatly modified or even canceled by the second Directress; redress of wrongs sought from the third Directress because she was "young and more understanding," while the third Directress, loving Sister Madeleine as she did, had still to uphold Sister Baptista as the properly constituted authority in this case.

She therefore always advised obedience to her directives and defended her granted permissions. Thus Sister Catherine was in a bind, caught up in petty crises which, as we all know, are to be found in all walks of life, but still wear one down to the breaking point. She did not yet have (at twenty-six years of age) the wisdom that can come only from first-hand experience and which, in middle age, she was to have in such abundance.

She had romped through life a free, blithe spirit; now she had to learn the meaning of our Lord's words that one can imitate Him only if she takes up her cross daily, and willingly. Sister Catherine was willing enough, but she had not as yet learned to accept the fact that even holy people—what with the complications and contradictions of tainted human nature—can bewilder our hearts and shake our faith, when they seem to ignore the demands of charity. Only in the next world would perfection be achieved and sustained, but this was the here and now and Sister Catherine had to deal with it; and she was nearer to the breaking point than anyone guessed.

It was just when the darkest hour seemed to promise a bright dawn that Sister Catherine received word that her dearly beloved father had been killed in a car accident. Now this was something Sister could readily accept. It involved no clash of personalities; it was simply something she could calmly accept as the will of God— something that, in perfect peace and resignation, she could discuss in the Chapel with Him heart to heart.

The next morning at breakfast, Sister Catherine sat white and listless at the table. The Sister-Infirmarian's professional, knowing eye recognized the signs and reached Sister Catherine just in time to prevent her from falling to the floor. All the Sisters of this large mission had heard the announcement in the Chapel that the Mass would be offered for the repose of the soul of Mr. Dennis Sullivan, father of Sister Catherine. Naturally everyone, including the province superiors, thought the fainting spell was due to shock at her father's sudden and violent death, and great was the sympathy of each Sister in the house.

But the practiced eye of Sister Rose Bohm, the Infirmarian, knew there was something deeper and, after a few days in the Seminary infirmary, insisted that Sister Catherine be removed to the larger and better equipped infirmary of the Sisters on mission in the hospital, in another part of the house.

Sister Eugenia Fealy, first Visitatrix (provincial superior), visited Sister Catherine each day, her penetrating eye searching for improvement. Sister Catherine parried all questions concerning the cause of her illness with "I am not really sick, but very tired." Sister Eugenia was shrewd, intuitive, and sharply perceptive. It would not be too much to hazard a theory that she guessed, at least partially, the cause of Sister Catherine's illness. It was Sister Eugenia's suggestion that Sister Catherine be transferred completely away from the temporary provincial house to St. Joseph Hospital, Alton, Illinois, a half-hour's trip from St. Louis.

The Sisters at Alton lovingly welcomed Sister Catherine, now well enough to be up most of the day. But the Sisters, always facing a nurse-shortage, were very busy all day long, so that Sister Catherine was left pretty much alone in the Community Room reading—of all things—*The Lives of our Deceased Sisters*. In a way, it sounds rather a morbid therapy, since "The Lives" insinuated that these departed Sisters had somehow attained to sanctity in their infancy, and few of us can identify with that phenomenon.

Since Sister Catherine retired immediately after supper, she had no recreational contact with the Sisters. But here a very revealing trait, rather predominant among the Daughters of Charity towards their sick companions, manifests itself. Of course no Sister is permitted to leave sick patients, except for the briefest time when another Sister can replace her for the time being. But the administrator's schedule is subject to change without inconveniencing others. So, busy though she was, the Sister Servant, in this case Sister Zoe Schieswohl, would "just happen" to have a half hour or so "free" every morning about ten o'clock, and again in the afternoon just after three o'clock, and would slip into the Community Room and say: "Sister Catherine, I don't have a thing on my mind right this minute—except you. Why don't we play three games of checkers, and see if I can beat you two out of three?"

Sister Catherine loved this "half hour" which stretched to an hour on days when Sister Zoe thought she looked unusually wan. They both played a good and very close game. Sister Catherine had had long years of practice playing chess with her father back in the cozy days of Texarkana, so she won more often than not, but only after Sister Zoe had put forth strenuous effort, in order to give challenge to her eager partner. Sister Zoe was a beautiful woman, with flashing brown eyes and cherry-red cheeks. She was generally, throughout the Community, considered "strict"—whatever that meant in those days, but her kind of therapy for Sister

Catherine revealed a loving heart. Though she has been dead for many, many years, I still blow her an occasional kiss, destination Heaven, for the tender loving care she gave to Sister Catherine. But Sister Catherine's health did not improve.

Sister Eugenia Fealy, immersed in the time-consuming affairs of the evolving western province, which at that time stretched from Iowa to the state of Washington and from Lake Michigan to the Gulf of Mexico, still made time for visits with Sister Catherine to note her progress and to bring her news of the Seminary. Among the younger Sisters of the province, Sister Eugenia was rated as capable of "looking into your soul; she can read every thought while you're thinking it," they were fond of saying with a slight shiver.

If Sister Eugenia could look into Sister Catherine's mind and read any of her thoughts, she gave no sign. But, on a certain day late in 1911, Sister Eugenia did give her the stunning news that Sister Madeleine was given a year's leave of absence to go to Paris to study under the famous Soeur Chesnlong, Directress of the Seminary where candidates from many countries made their novitiate under her guidance. She is still spoken of reverently and considered, in the annals of the Community, a great Directress, judged mainly and rightly on the type of Sister she produced after one year's guidance. Sister Catherine smiled brightly at this piece of news. Now her beloved Sister Madeleine would be under the tutelage of a kindred mind and a brilliant example of what a Seminary Directress—for those long-gone distant times—should be.

But the greatest news Sister Eugenia brought on a fall day of 1912 was for Sister Catherine herself. "I am not satisfied with the progress you are making here," Sister Eugenia told her very kindly. "There's no place to walk or sit in the sun. I think, if you go to St. Mary's Hospital in Milwaukee for a few months, you will get more exercise walking along the shore of beautiful Lake Michigan. In that bracing climate you're bound to develop a bigger appetite and sleep better." Sister Catherine was deeply grateful for Sister Eugenia's kindness and said so. In a few days she traveled to St. Mary's in Milwaukee with an invalid Sister, who was to spend the rest of her life there.

Even sixty years ago, in buildings long since replaced and added to again, St. Mary's Hospital, Milwaukee, was a thing of beauty which boasted, "Every room looks out upon the Lake"—and in summer the lake was as blue as the Mediterranean. But the rooms in the Sisters' quarters had no view of the lake and were located on the fourth floor far, far from where the action was.

Sister Catherine and her companion, Sister Frances McKenney, were welcomed with that same warm cordiality that St. Vincent insisted upon and made a matter of Rule, way back in 1633. While autumn lasted and when the weather was briskly cool, Sister Catherine took long, long walks on the sandy, rock-bound shore that stretched as far as one could see. Sometimes she just sat on one of the small boulders that dotted the shore. But the appetite did not get bigger, nor did Sister Catherine's health get any better. One boon, however, was the companionship of Sister Frances McKenney who, confined to a wheel chair, sewed, embroidered, and turned out exquisite needlework. Sister Catherine, in spite of her daily handiwork in sewing torn dresses and incorrigible hems back in school at

Shreveport, was always clumsy with a needle, but she was good company for Sister Frances.

With true Sisterly kindness, the Sister Servant arranged each day that Sister Catherine would eat a very early supper, anticipate her night prayers, and go to bed at five o'clock. "It will be so nice and quiet," Sister Dolores Gillespie told her, "so you will have a good long night's sleep and be fresh as a daisy by five in the morning," which was an extra hour, since the Sisters at that time in history, rose at four o'clock. Sister Frances' room was on the first floor, so there was no one to talk to, no one within call. This was when Sister Catherine's too lively imagination took over.

Speaking of this period years later to a close and trusted friend, who at the time was going through a painful illness, Sister Catherine recalled her own experience: "Oh, those dreadful twilights of early to bed at dusk! Sister, I would crawl into bed and lie there in stark terror! I couldn't put my finger on a thing that I was afraid of, but I would lie there frozen with a nameless dread. To this day, I recall those nights—those very dark nights of the soul—when I could only cry with David:

> Heal me, O Lord, for my body is in terror;
> My soul, too, is utterly terrified;

"So you see, Sister," she would add, "it is a universal experience that goes back to the beginning of man. Nurses always watch for 'apprehensiveness' in their patients. They know it is worse than sickness itself."

"But why didn't you tell somebody?" her friend asked.

"Pride," she answered promply. "I was ashamed of

being such a coward, especially since everyone was so kind to me. It was a great concession on the part of Sister Dolores to send me so early to bed. She honestly thought that, if you could stand up, being with the Community was better than any kind of medicine."

"You said that terror came from your pride," her friend probed. "Didn't it go deeper than that?"

Sister Catherine paused. "Frankly, yes, Sister. My imagination used to run wild with a very concrete fear, which was partly responsible for my not getting well in Alton. You see, I had read everything I could lay my hands on about the requirements of the religious life; and over and over again in various pamphlets, three signs were given to identify a vocation: 1) good health; 2) average intelligence; 3) acceptance by a religious congregation.

"In the pamphlets I read, 'good health' was always placed first. The implication was that, if your health failed, especially before you made your Holy Vows, that was 'a sign from God' that you did not belong in the religious life and would be sent home."

With the freedom that can exist only between friends who have weathered storms together, she related the situation—which has been described in previous pages— and went on to say: "I know my nerves were shattered then, but I do think I would have recovered in a reasonable time, if I had not been convinced that I was in great danger of being sent home because of ill health."

Since her friend had experienced the same fear for the first ten years of her Community life, she knew exactly how Sister Catherine had felt. It is a ridiculous idea, not an iota of common sense to support the fear, since the Community has never sent a Sister home solely because her health fails. Sister Catherine knew this well; she had been on duty in the Seminary and had seen for herself that the Community uses the criterion of "good health" as a prerequisite for entrance— not for perseverance. If they accept a candidate who is not strong, they accept her for life.

Analyzing the heartbreaking "terror" and the unreasonable "fears," one cannot escape the temptation to believe that at least a small remnant of little Maudie Summerfield's over-active imagination was fighting for its life. But in this case, unlike Maudie, weeping over her own death and detailed burial, there were no healing tears to act as a catharsis for her terror and fears.

But a beautiful (and enlightening) rainbow was just around the corner.

FOUR

It was in August of 1912 that Sister Catherine received a letter—a special one—from Sister Eugenia, telling her again that she was concerned as to what would be the next best step to bring about Sister Catherine's restoration to complete health. "You have a fine constitution, really," Sister Eugenia wrote, "and I know that in God's own time He will make you perfectly well, so do not be discouraged at this test of your love of God." Sister Catherine's heart soared as these words allayed her fears. But there was more to come.

"Just as an experiment, dear Sister," wrote Sister Eugenia, "I would very much like you to go over to St. Rose's Home for a few hours each day to teach the seventh and eighth grades. I know it will be new to you at first, to teach thirty children; but I also know you have a good head and a tender heart—two essential qualities for teachers.

"In this same mail I am notifying Sister Dolores. Please let me know how you feel about this assignment."

Sister Catherine wrote that she would be delighted, as she would have written if the letter were sending her to darkest Africa. But, with Wordsworth, her heart really did leap up as though she were beholding a host of daffodils. But this was something much more substantial than daffodils, or all the flowers of the world.

The perceptive reader will see that at last a root cause of Sister Catherine's long illness was coming to light.

1

St. Rose's Home for Girls was a large red-brick building whose location depended upon which door you used in leaving St. Mary's Hospital. Seen from the front door, it was adjacent to the Hospital, with a narrow side street between. Viewed from the side door, it was directly across the street—meaning this same little side street. Like the hospital, it faced lovely Lake Michigan, with easy access to the shore where the children and Sisters of St. Rose's often in summer ate their evening meal and on holidays had picnics. The children loved to wade in the lake and delighted in bucking the sometime high waves.

At first Sister Catherine continued to live at the hospital and go to school "across the street" each morning. But, early in 1913, she received word from St. Louis that she was "missioned" to St. Rose's as a full time teacher—which gave her a real sense of belonging. She had, at long last, joined the ranks of the fully employed.

Sister Catherine was ecstatically happy at St. Rose's. Sister Jerome Bress, the Sister Servant, was a large, plump, good-natured person. Most of the Sisters were, like Sister Catherine, still in their twenties and, although the children were not easy to handle, Sister Catherine remembered that "Madeleine Sullivan" had been in that category at school, too. She easily won their respect first, and then their love, because of her understanding and strong sense of humor.

But the climax of joy for Sister Catherine was that she was now in a position where her duty did not only "permit" but *required* reading in every academic field. Real reading, beyond the necrologies of sainted Sisters who seemed never to have had any conflicts or difficulties on the road to sanctity, since they had been born to holiness and manifested it in their cradles.

There were outside readings assigned in the biographies of great historical figures (shades of Sister Gabriel and Napoleon); there were poets and their poetry, and essays by the critics, favorable or unfavorable to their works. There were assignments in geography, with supplementary readings in the *National Geographic;* there were anthologies of literature; and finally, her eleven and twelve year old pupils were reading *David Copperfield, Great Expectations, Sam Weller's Valentine,* and *Stories from the Old Testament.* All the children of the four upper grades joined Sister Catherine's Reading Club.

2

One day Sister Jerome called Sister Catherine into her office. "Sister," she said, after seating her comfortably in a chair close to her own, "I want to thank you for the interest in books you have aroused in all the students of the house, as well as your own class, and leading them to realize how important education is to their future lives when they will have to earn their own living. You are a born teacher and you have infected everybody with your enthusiasm. But this new interest in their classwork has played havoc with their house duties. The girls who have the responsibility of keeping the parlors swept and well dusted are now pulling the shades down, to hide the dust and dirt, and are crouching behind the sofas and easy chairs, *reading*. I admit that their interest in books has greatly improved their conduct, both in and out of the classroom, but these children are not going to grow into ladies of leisure with time to read for hours and hours every day. Are we, perhaps, spoiling them for the more practical things in life?"

Sister Catherine was alarmed. The girls were so happy with their new-found joy in the world of books, their behaviour had so improved that life was easier for all of the other teachers. The girls too were getting vicarious experiences that would mature them, make them cultured women, build wide vocabularies which they could gain in no other way. She put all this into words for Sister Jerome, whose own taste in reading ran largely to *Christian Perfection, True Devotion to Mary,* and *The Conferences and Letters of St. Vincent de Paul.*

They came to a happy compromise. Sister Catherine knew absolutely nothing about housework, but pledged that the girls would finish their domestic duties first, take at least a half hour of exercise in the open air, and then, and then only, could they read. It was an eloquent appeal. Sister Catherine left Sister Jerome's office with a fifty-dollar bill to be used for selecting new books for the library.

Sister Catherine steadily improved in health. She used to say of St. Rose's, "It was a little bit of Heaven. There was perfect harmony among the Sisters; we were all pretty much the same age and we had loads of fun. Evening recreation (in schools there is no time for a midday recreation period) was uproarious, and I think Sister Jerome enjoyed it as much or even more than those of us who made veritable fools of ourselves—all for the honor and glory of God." Sister Catherine kept in touch with the companions of that day, even when they were scattered over the province on different missions.

3

The influence Sister Catherine exercised over the girls at St. Rose's was phenomenal. Many of them corresponded with her for years, and a few up to the very end of Sister's life. Some of their letters she kept in her files. There is one very touching letter from a young woman of thirty. It reads in part:

> You are always very near me, Sister, and it is certainly a red letter day when I receive a letter from you. Even though you know I have not been, and am not even now, a good person, the knowledge of your faithful friendship often keeps me from going further down the drain.
>
> But I want to confide something very special to your heart, trusting you to understand that I am trying to go straight now. It was just ten nights ago. I was in deep trouble. You can guess what. I was so depressed at the complete betrayal of someone I had loved and trusted and honestly believed that he loved me too.
>
> I simply could not stand my own company a minute longer. Though I was in bed and it was nearly midnight, I got up and dressed and went for a walk. Don't faint. I am, more's the pity, used to being on the street at midnight. You know my background, Sister, so what

can you expect? I remember when I'd say that to you, you would say, so confidently: "Just hold fast to your faith in God; remember you are captain of your own soul." Sister, I'm afraid you just don't know how hard it is to be good in the kind of world I live in.

Well, anyhow, I walked and walked, and I headed straight for the river. The sides of the bridge are rather low, and I sat on the top rail for fifteen minutes, thinking. I could see no way out of my problem, so I got ready to jump. I thought to myself, "God has forgotten me; He really doesn't even remember me, it is so long since I deserted Him."

Sister, I actually put one foot over the railing. Oddly enough, I wasn't scared to die. I was in Hell right now —surely the other one couldn't be any worse than this. And I wasn't afraid of the dark waters below. So I was just about to put the other foot over without any fear in my heart. But suddenly your face appeared before me. I could see it as plainly as when I sat in the front desk in your classroom and—let me say it, please— adored you.

You seemed to be saying to me, "Oh, Clare, can you do this to our Lord?" I said, angrily, "Yes, I can," stubborn like always. Then I looked into your eyes—has anyone ever told you how blue they are?—and then, bursting into tears, I said to you: "But I can't do it to you! You were the one who taught me to love to read— and saved me from hours of loneliness. And Sister, we all loved you because you never used to lecture us or preach at us!"

I climbed back over the railing of the bridge and went home. The next morning I wrote to the Mayor and told him the rails of this bridge were too low, a danger, especially to children.

The writer was with Sister Catherine when she received and read this letter. What did Sister Catherine do? Well, she wept briefly; then set the wheels in motion to get this young woman a good social worker in New York, a Sister in whom Sister Catherine had great confidence and knew she would see Clare through her trouble.

4

An interesting sidelight on this letter is that Sister Catherine had taught composition to Clare for two years, encouraging her to try to become a writer. It didn't work out that way, but what a talent for writing!

Pages could be filled with excerpts of letters from former girls of St. Rose's. But space is too limited. However, for those who might wonder how Clare turned out at last, there is a very interesting angle. She had a child, and Sister Catherine encouraged her to give it up for adoption in a wonderful Catholic home. Then Sister persuaded Clare to choose a spiritual director from among the names of three priests located in New York who were personal friends over a period of years. The one Clare chose (because she liked his name) was a pastor in downstate New York, who gave her a job as his secretary. One day Father saw an ad in the morning newspaper, asking for a fairly young woman to act as companion for an elderly but very alert lady. Father suggested that Clare apply. She was shocked: "With my background, Father! Who would give me a reference?" Father replied gallantly: "I will. You've worked for me three years now. Let bygones be bygones. Hasn't our Lord said: 'Though your sins be as scarlet, amen I say to you, I shall not remember them'?"

The stunning climax is that, at Father's suggestion, Clare visited the woman in person, after first writing a letter. She found her future employer a very wealthy, old woman, but rather brusque at first meeting. At the end of a two hour session during which they spoke of many things—omitting cabbages and sealing wax but including kings—the dear old lady's eyes smiled softly at Clare as she said: "Out of seven applicants, I choose you. Not only because of Father Lyon's wonderful rec-ommendation, which is fine, but I'd expect a woman of thirty-five to settle down with all her foolishness be-hind her. No, I chose you mainly because your own letter to me was so well written and, my dear, you know how to carry on a good conversation, and you are well-read. I foresee some very good times ahead exchanging views on books."

Sister Catherine was overjoyed with this news from Clare. She said to the writer: "I do believe all my guilt feelings about reading have been exorcised. I wish that I could show this letter to Sister Jerome, God rest her soul." "Why not send it to Sister Gabriel Murtagh?" her companion suggested. To this wicked suggestion there was no response.

5

On March 15, 1914, Sister Catherine made her first Holy Vows. She was radiantly happy. Her health was much improved, and all her fears of being sent home had vanished. She felt *all* Daughter of Charity now; her vocation was dearer to her than life itself. She could now be happy that she, by the grace of God, had come through that rough period of fear and terror without once thinking of taking back what had so whole-heartedly been given to God. And now, today—March 15, 1914—she made a complete oblation of herself to our Lord, and she felt a deep sense of peace and security.

Speaking of this time much later, Sister Catherine said to a friend: "My Holy Vows released me forever from those silly, groundless fears that I would be sent home. But you know the devil is very tricky, very subtle. He even made me feel that I ought to go home of my own accord, since I was sick so long and doing nothing for the Community. And I recall my sister, Elizabeth, like Job's friends, visiting me at the time, urging me to come home. She would say: 'You can see that this is really a time when God is speaking to you, showing you that this is not your vocation. If it were, you would not have broken down with an illness that has no name.'"

"She meant this advice in all kindness and was shocked when I said, 'Elizabeth, be still. Help me to implore God to keep me, not to let me be sent home.' Elizabeth was amazed to hear me talk like this. One is always such a 'pearl of great price' to one's own family. She thought the whole Community should be on its collective knees, thanking God for having sent this gem to adorn the Order. But I am grateful to God," she repeated, "for those hard times; and I am thankful to Sister Augustine Park for working at least a little iron into my backbone. It helped to bring me through—though hardly with flying colors."

There was no cloud in her sky to warn her of rougher days ahead. Saints are not turned out in assembly lines, but cooperation with Providence in whatever He sends to try one's soul—or to purify it from its faults—strengthens us to do what we came to do, *follow Christ,* and to carry our cross as we follow the hard road He trod.

6

Another two years flew by at St. Rose's. Sister Catherine had no idea that 1916 was to be a strangely momentous year for her; but lightning did not strike for five years. While Sister Catherine was enthusiastically carrying on her teaching duties, loving her work more and more as the days went by, the local mailman, making his daily rounds, brought sorrow to this one today and joy to her tomorrow. One special letter arrived one bright morning for Sister Jerome, the Sister Servant at St. Rose's. In her kindness she stopped by Sister Catherine's classroom where she was preparing assignments for the day. Sister Jerome read her a paragraph of the letter which was from the provincial house in St. Louis. It said in part:

> I am happy to tell you that among the Sisters privileged to make the annual retreat at the provincial house in this year of 1916 is Sister Catherine Sullivan. Please have her arrive in St. Louis a few days ahead of time so she can rest and relax a little before entering her retreat.

Sister Catherine's cup of joy was overflowing. Every Sister in the province waited eagerly for her "turn" to make a retreat at the Provincial House which came about every three or four years. In due time she arrived in St. Louis, two days ahead of time, which she spent visiting with Sisters from the other missions, and above all, her beloved Sister Madeleine with whom she walked over the beautiful grounds for the two free evenings she had.

It is customary when making a retreat at the provincial house to have a half hour interview with the Visitatrix (Sister Eugenia Fealy) who was remarkable for getting thoroughly well acquainted with the Sisters of her province. Sister Catherine's turn for a visit happened to come the morning before retreat closed. Sister Eugenia was genuinely pleased with the progress Sister Catherine had made and the really miraculous success she had achieved in teaching.

Sister Catherine used to recall this conversation when the topic turned to the subject of teaching versus nursing. "This is what Sister Eugenia said to me—and she was not given to paying compliments:"

> At last, at long last, dear Sister Catherine, you have truly found yourself. I know it must have been a great sacrifice for you to give up nursing, but look what a teacher you are! I am sure that St. Rose's is just the place for you now, and future assignments should be in the teaching field. You are a born teacher, and you must never forget to thank God for the talents He has given you.

Sister Catherine reeled out of the room, overcome with the compliments and the assurance that God makes His Will known through her superiors. This conversation took place about nine o'clock in the morning. At ten-thirty the next morning (after mail delivery), the Sisters heard the special bell that was rung when the Council was to meet. In those days, when the bell rang, each Sister knelt for a short time to beg the Holy Spirit to direct the decisions the Council would be called upon to make for the well-being of the province. Recalling this particular day, which Sister Catherine did frequently, she used to remark: "That day, instead of praying for the decisions *to* be made, I thanked God for the one that *had* been made about my future as a teacher."

At one-thirty, Sister Catherine was summoned to Sister Eugenia, who was sitting at the head of the Council table. Sister Catherine sensed that something was wrong, very wrong, as she seated herself at the right side of Sister Eugenia at the table. "Sister," began Sister Eugenia, "I never like to reverse a decision once it has been made; that is why I usually wait until the last moment to tell a Sister that she is missioned." There was a slight tremor in her voice as she continued. "This morning's mail brought news of an emergency at the Leprosarium at Carville. Dear Sister, I meant every word I said yesterday morning, but now I have to tell you that your services as a nurse are desperately needed. And the worst of it is you will have to leave at three o'clock today. You will have a companion." Sister Catherine knew that Sister Eugenia felt as disappointed as she, herself, did. Sister Catherine smiled as though she had been the recipient of good news. "We can always count on Sister Augustine Parks' 'soldiers'," Sister Eugenia said with a twinkle in her eye. She embraced Sister Catherine warmly as she bade her goodby.

FIVE

Sister Catherine Sullivan arrived in Carville early in 1916, the sixteenth Sister to be assigned to this work. One can judge of the primitive state of the colony, since a Sister there observed with pride:

> The patients numbered 103 at this time, and the same year marked the installation of electric lights to replace candles and kerosene lamps. Plans were being made to purchase a cinematograph for the entertainment of the patients.

The Community, at this period, was in the throes of changing the "Leper Colony" into a State Hospital and, finally, to the federal institution it is today. But there were difficulties in securing just the right place—Louisiana was not happy to cede land for what most of its people considered a dread purpose. To look back a moment, the first world war impeded progress, but finally the federally owned and operated hospital was officially opened on February 1 (note the date) 1921, with Dr. Oswald E. Denney as its first medical officer in charge. Present at the hoisting of "Old Glory" were Sister Edith, Sister Servant, Sister DeChantal, Sister Catherine Sullivan, Father Keenan, Doctor and Mrs. Oswald Denney.

Sister Catherine had a way of remarking at odd times that once each year one passed the date that sometime in the future would be called "the day God sounded the call for the beginning of eternity." But February 1, 1921 gave no hint of that "last day," February 1, 1969. We were still to have our dear Sister for forty-nine years.

The Sisters, who served as the nursing staff, and Dr. Denney were remarkably interested in improving physical facilities. Hand in hand with the medical and nursing staff's great progress in understanding Hansen's disease and its scientific care, beautiful, functional buildings sprang up in a veritable southern plantation setting—live oaks with heavy masses of Spanish moss adding to their beauty. Each patient who wished it could have a plot of ground for gardening, and finally "resort cottages" were built where patients could enjoy "vacations."

1

Sister Catherine had one special project to which she gave every moment she could spare from her nursing duties, and that was the building of a beautiful Chapel for the Catholic patients, who at the present time had to crowd into an old relic of a slave cabin for services; while the Protestants had a very well built brick church, erected by the generous members of the varying denominations. Sister Catherine felt that nowhere could the Catholic patients find more solace and comfort than in the solitude and silence of their very own Chapel where they could speak to God of their sorrows and needs.

With characteristic physical vigor and spiritual zeal, she set about doing the things that she could do— using the rare gifts that God had given her to reach

71

out into the hearts of those who would be touched with the plight of the human condition and needs of the patients at Carville.

She gave talks to local and farther away organizations in New Orleans, even as far away as Chicago and California. She presented to her audiences the true picture of Hansen's disease (so called after Dr. Hansen who was the first to isolate the bacilli that caused leprosy), showing how the patients were suffering from a 6,000 year old prejudice nourished by old wives' tales; of how the patients were in a state of contagious decay, whereas; in the vast number of cases, patients lived many years without any blemish that could be detected except by the most perceptive of doctors.

2

She spoke of the need for a Chapel; she wrote articles and appeared before many audiences who found her logical presentation of Hansen's disease irresistible. The following article, which Sister Catherine cut down to leaflet size, alone brought in more than ten thousand dollars toward the building of the Chapel. That was considered a large sum in the 1920's.

THE LONGEST MILE IN THE WORLD

Sister Catherine

Abbe Dimnet quotes a little boy ("Out of the mouths of babes") as saying gravely to his elders: "You look at what I am looking at but you do not see what I see." So, many a chance visitor to the National Home for Lepers, at Carville, Louisiana, sees only its vast expanse of well-kept lawns and well-built homes. Interested physicians see a Class A Hospital, with every scientific device for the probing of human ills and every modern appliance for the relief of physical pain. Astounded sociologists see an ideal city, in miniature, where every civic problem has been worked out, by the three hundred and fifty patients who form its citizenry, to a satisfactory conclusion. But one whom no number of trees can blind to a forest, sees in the beautiful reservation, only the longest Mile in the World. A Mile beginning at the entrance gate and ending in a grass-grown slope just out of sight of the buildings. A Mile, walked with joy, by a man in health, in twenty minutes: A Mile negotiated haltingly and with much agony, by one who bears the burden of leprosy, in twenty years. A Mile that is only an incident to him who walks it because he will and not because he must; a Mile that is a tragedy to him who walks it because he must and not because he will.

Averaging admissions to the leprosarium, every sixth day of the year, some one begins anew that Mile's momentous journey. "Some one." Keep that softly in mind, for only too often the frenzied fear aroused by the "leper" blinds the hearers to the simplest and truest definition of the word that was ever given: "A leper is a man—husband, father, brother or son—or a woman—wife, mother, daughter or sister—who is entitled to more than common consideration because of his or her uncommon affliction." Standing just outside the inviting whitewashed lodge gate, let us note the participants in the entering procession. Men predominate, for to every woman whose feet Fate has set along that Mile, we count two men.

Today, it is a young man, an ex-soldier, who has served his country well. He has now a harder fight ahead of him, for he battles a treacherous foe who gives no quarter and has never known a conqueror. Next comes a woman, young in years, and with post-partum weakness yet upon her. Six weeks ago, she and her stalwart Acadian husband, in their home along the bayou in the Teche country of Louisiana, looked happily forward to the coming of their first babe. It was the wife's first meeting with one of the medical fraternity. Carefully, the doctor examined the dark splotches to which the young wife had given no attention. His trained eye knew only too well their significance. So the baby which was to have brought joy, brought dark despair instead. "Another one," a grey-haired man says chokingly, as he greets the Doctor in charge. "Another one" means that his third and last son has come to join his two brothers who preceded him to the leprosarium. And ever, in the ears of those who heard it, will sound that father's anguished cry: "Would to God that I had leprosy that I might stay with my children." It is common for relatives to walk that Mile together; brothers and sisters—six, seven and even eight in one family—mother and children, cousins sometimes closely, sometimes distantly related. But by an enigma which remains a medical mystery but not a social mercy, rarely, very, very rarely indeed, do husband and wife go down that way together.

Even the dancing feet of little children are found along that Mile. A burly policeman conducts thither his little daughter, a child of seven years. "I am taking you to a new school, girlie," he had beguiled her with, as they left their home. The new school sounds fascinating, but as the great gate is about to clang and the father attempts a goodbye kiss, a prophetic terror convulses the little one and she cries out: "Daddy, I don't like this school. Take me away." And the officer of the law, who a week before had been commended for special valor, is unable to undo the clutch of those tiny fingers. Ah, how often is that little one's prayer repeated by her fellow travelers: "Heavenly Father, this school is hard indeed, and I cannot bear it. Take me away." Yes, "take me away" tho it be no further than to the grass-grown slope at the end of the Mile.

It is something of a temptation to insert more excerpts of Sister Catherine's writing during these years, but Sister Catherine's life was a long one. To do it justice, one would have to accept a three-volume study; but this would be unwieldy and perhaps the aim of this book would not be achieved, which is best expressed in what might have been the sub-title of this work: "How Sister Catherine became a Saint." To do that one must dwell on human relationships rather than on special achievements.

3

One day at noon recreation the sound of the bell announcing "someone in the parlor—wants a tour" reached the Community Room where the Sisters were assembled for a half hour's relaxation.

"Any volunteer?" asked Sister Edith, knowing that it was a long tiring walk.

The Sisters all looked at Sister Catherine, one of them remarking, "You're the one with the gift of gab." Sister Catherine smiled, knowing well that this was a dodge they used often to escape the chore.

"Be sure to put in a plug for our Chapel," one Sister teasingly called after her, "who knows?"

In the parlor Sister Catherine found a rather dusty, travel-weary priest and greeted him cordially.

"I've always been intrigued with this place, Sister, but I've never been able until today to see it for myself. Will you show me round and tell me about—well, just everything."

Sister Catherine smiled with interest. "It's a Cook's tour," she warned, as they started out. "Tell me when you're tired."

They covered the patients' quarters, and Father's outgoing easy way of meeting people charmed the patients that gathered around him, and one of them said: "You haven't told us Father's name, Sister Catherine."

Sister's face flushed a little. "I'm sorry, but I honestly don't know it—"

The guest interrupted, "Oh, just call me Father. Shakespeare says, 'What's in a name anyhow?'" As they walked back to the convent part of the Colony, Father pointed to a parcel of land roped off with a sign that said: "Site of future Catholic Chapel." He paused with a quickening sense of interest. "Tell me about this, Sister Catherine."

Speaking of this at a much later period, Sister Catherine said, "I never put my 'gift of gab' to better use." When she had finished telling him about the Chapel, he asked her what she was doing about raising funds for this project. As they were in Sister Catherine's little home-made "publicity office," she handed him several leaflets in which she described the need for a Catholic Chapel.

"Say," he said, "I can help you—I not only can but I will. I can do three things right away: first, I can give you money now and can help you find a way to raise more; second, I can get you invitations all over the states to talk on your favorite subject, Hansen's disease, and how much these Catholic patients need a Chapel, a place of solace of their own." He hesitated just a moment. "And thirdly, I offer you a forum in *Church Extension Magazine*, for spreading the good news of better days to come."

Sister Catherine could only gasp: "Why YOU'RE Bishop McGuinness of Church Extension!"

In later years, in relating this encounter, she would say: "Dear Sisters, Providence walks abroad each day of the year. Always remember that when you are tempted to go to the parlor reluctantly. Our Lord Himself might be waiting there for you. Look what happened to me!"

In God's good time, as Sister Catherine was wont to say, the Chapel was built, a perfect gem of simplicity and quiet beauty. But to whomsoever much is given, of him much will be required. Success has a way of demanding sometimes colossal compensation. Sister Catherine was no exception, either to the human rule or to its supernatural counterpart.

4

There was to be, in Sister Catherine's life, another dark night, although Sister Catherine was wont to say throughout her Community life that God had never asked her to bear any cross big enough to label "suffering." Well, we all have different names for our woes, but most of us know, by reflection and actual experience, how true Thoreau's dictum is when he said: "All men lead lives of quiet desperation." But, to "tell it like it is," we must go back a little in the history of our Community to one Sister who had exercised much influence on Sister Catherine, who in turn practically underwent an amazing change in personality and character under Sister Catherine's influence. But, at the time of which we write, neither had been acquainted with the other except by hearsay.

Sister Martha Lawlor was a most unusual person, and —dare we say it aloud—unusual persons are not exactly "favorites" either in the outside world or in religious Communities. Especially, if God in His own secret designs, gave them great intellectual powers. America reserves her applause for do-ers of the deed, the activists who are more known for their hard work than for their powers of clear thinking. Rarely are intellectuals endowed with both qualities: a love of the things of the mind, and a love of purposeful action.

But Sister Martha was one of the rare exceptions. She had her R.N. at the time she entered the Community and was highly respected as a most unusually gifted nurse. Sister Martha's intellectual preoccupation was centered on her profession: nursing, newest and best procedures in all aspects of medicine and patient care. Now all this is admirable, but, in each hospital where Sister Martha worked, it was rumored that she was a medical doctor. This rumor started when internes, residents and older doctors would say of her, in passing, "Best doctor on the staff. Best *man* we've got in surgery and research." It has been said that the medical profession has the highest record for professional jealousy. One wonders what research has been made on the subject or what high class opinion polls have been taken to prove this statement.

It was all the more remarkable that Sister Martha should be professionally a controversial figure, because she was a withdrawn sort of person, not a good mixer, except in the case of doctors of experience who had reached the top and were no longer threatened with competition. But top men of the medical profession had a way of seeking her out, at various hospital conventions and meetings, where she was quite vocal. They would ask her opinion, listen to her theories with respect, and often, when in the city where she was on mission, would visit with her to their mutual benefit.

But let us be honest in admitting what we all know: it is not easy, whether lay or religious, to have a prima donna—a broadly acknowledged prima donna—not to say a genius, working in close contact with you every day. Perhaps this is not an admirable trait of human nature, but then, let us not miss the fact (no one ever does) that the genius is not always an easy person to live with, and, often without her being fully aware of it, brings upon herself, by her manner, her life-style, her method of work, suspicion and distrust. The first, though hardly the worst, is the accusation that the prima donna seeks the limelight for herself alone—not for the Community to whom she gave her life to serve; nor for God to whom she dedicated all her powers and capabilities, to prove her love. No, she is a seeker after popularity, aggressive in her search for fame.

5

Anyone who knew Sister Martha, and had a spark of perception, would never accuse her of "showing off" or seeking applause. But, to St. Paul's statement that there are not many who are noble, we can add with even more truth, there are not many who are perceptive, nor are there many who can reject unsupported prejudice. So, in the life of Sister Martha Lawlor, rumor begot rumors, and legends blew up to enormous size. Perhaps an example of my contact with her will help to explain.

It was in August of 1920. We were returning from St. Louis to our missions in Louisiana after our annual retreat. Sister Martha sat beside me in the smoky train that was carrying us home. I felt quite honored to have Sister Martha in the seat beside me. We talked all day. I was eager to know her, to become a friend of hers. I was twenty-one at the time, and Sister must have been about forty-five, but we felt no generation gap. To me she exuded a sincere but inoffensive humility. There was nothing of Uriah Heep about her, just a genuine humility encompassed within a framework of simplicity. I was fascinated with her, more so with her spiritual outlook than even with her sort of shy sense of humor that I found delightful.

She gave me an opening that, in the back of my mind, I had been waiting for. We had been talking about ourselves, sharing little confidences that sometimes come easier with a comparative stranger than with a friend. I had just confided to her that I was going to make my first Holy Vows in November of that year, and how I felt about it. She had remarked that she herself seemed to have no lasting dwelling place, since she seldom lasted more than a few years on her many missions, which included even Panama.

"Oh," I said, with the wisdom so peculiar to the young. (I was then twenty-one.) "Don't you think that's because you're the kind of person around whom legends grow? And really, as the word implies, not always true."

She smiled a little thoughtfully. "Legends are not always lies either. There is usually a grain of truth, isn't there?"

I hesitated for a moment. Then I said, "Sister Martha, there are only two of these legends about you that interest me—and I think they're lies. Would you think me terribly rude to ask you about them?"

She turned toward me with a gleam of interest in her eye: "Tell me," she said.

"Well, Sister," I replied . . . "there are only two legends which really intrigue me, and I want to ask you if they are true. The first is that once you had to have an operation for appendicitis, and you refused to take an anaesthetic, because you wanted to stay awake and direct the entire operation. So, in spite of what must have been excruciating pain, you directed your surgery in every detail. Is that true?"

"Yes, it is true," she said with almost a sad smile. "I did not have full confidence in the surgeon, and, when I asked his permission, he said, 'Yes, you'll be a source of confidence to me'. But, Sister, I'm not proud of that episode. I was young," she said reminiscently, "and rash."

I looked at her with admiration. "Were you clobbered for it?"

She smiled ruefully: "Yes, I was clobbered. I deserved it, because it is unethical for a nurse to attempt to tell a doctor what to do—and, anyhow, very few of them listen anyway."

While I was digesting this, she asked with ill-concealed amusement, "What is the second rumor? You see, one was really true."

"Well, the next 'legend'" I said, burning with interest, "is that once you were assisting a surgeon who was operating on a woman and you thought he was needlessly removing some healthy tissue. You gasped in horror, and said, 'Oh, Doctor, don't go in there'. He threw the scalpel down and said, 'Well, Sister Martha,' almost beside himself with anger, 'you finish the job'—and hurried from the room. There was no time to lose, so you picked up the instruments and went right on with the operation, finished sewing the woman up—then you, too, left the operating room almost exhausted. But the top man in surgery congratulated you that same afternoon."

Sister smiled at me. "You're right about this rumor, too. I should not have said a word during the operation, or at any other time. But I don't feel so sorry about this as I do about the other. This time my conscience and sense of justice were affronted. I'm glad I interrupted what he was doing; he knew it was wrong. Still," she added judicially, "I had again failed seriously in the ethics of my profession."

I loved Sister Martha from that moment until she died some sixteen years later.

This saga of Sister Martha Lawlor will perhaps seem irrelevant to some readers, but she figures so dramatically in the life of Sister Catherine's second "night" that it seems important for the reader to get a telling insight into the kind of person she was.

6

Life at Carville was flourishing under the federal government, which in the way of finances left nothing undone for brightening the life—as far as one can—for those afflicted with Hansen's disease. Sister Catherine was far ahead of these anti-intellectual times. She sent Sister Hilary Ross to nearby Louisiana State University (across the river) to earn a degree in chemistry. Sister Hilary was a born scientist. She was placed in charge of the laboratory and gave her time to research: studying blood changes, symptoms of increase or decrease in the health of the patients where the condition of the blood played an important role. Sister Hilary collaborated on various vital articles with the various doctors who were interested in research, and these articles—published in learned journals of medicine, particularly *The National Journal of Leprosy*—not only made the United States Public Health Hospital at Carville (the only one in the United States) internationally known, but helped doctors to diagnose and treat the disease in its early stages.

Dr. Denney was extremely well pleased with the work the Sister-nurses were doing; pleased, too, with his medical and clerical staff and all was right with the world. The Sisters, unfettered before with many regulations, directives, and guidelines, now felt somewhat restricted, but, trained well in obedience in the Community, they saw that the federal government made prompt obedience a way of life. They often mar-

83

veled at the respectful obedience the under-officers gave their chief medical officer. "It was as if they, too, had vowed obedience," one Sister said.

Early in 1921, or perhaps it was the fall of that year, Sister Martha Lawlor was added to the Sister-staff at Carville. "Never in my life," she used to say later, "did I receive so warm a welcome as I did at Carville." And nowhere in the Community could Sister Martha make better use of her talents. Perhaps, too, she never had so faithful and loving a friend as she found in Sister Catherine, who was to have a profound influence on her character and personality.

Dr. Denney was not slow to see that he had a fine talent squad in his hospital, but Sister Martha was the bright and shining star of the nursing staff. Though not a Catholic, he respected the Sisters highly. But he never lost sight of the fact that he was the Commanding Officer. Until this time early in the spring of 1923, this was no problem, but the Sister Servant at that time was missioned and, in keeping with military protocol, Dr. Denney was the first to be told of the change. His reaction was that the appointment of her successor must be cleared through him. In almost peremptory use of his office, he wrote to St. Louis: "I want Sister Martha to be appointed Chief of Nursing Staff."

To the Community in St. Louis, this posed a problem, because in those days the Chief Nurse had to be (as a policy of the Community) the Sister Servant. Sister Eugenia wrote this to Dr. Denney and said that Sister Martha's talents lay in the professional field and not as a Community Superior, but she promised to send a very competent Sister Servant, who was also one of the best nurses in the Community. She explained that she did not like divided authority in a house and that the policy of the Community (remember this was almost fifty years ago) was that the Sister Servant be Chief Nurse. Sister Eugenia promised to send a Sister eminently qualified for both duties.

Of course, this was fuel to an already very hot flame. Dr. Denney sent off another of his fiery letters, saying something to the effect that he was the Commanding Officer, and he alone would select the Chief Nurse. "As for the naming of a superior, the Sister who is Chief Nurse will act in that capacity as in the past."

This was completely contrary to the policy of the Community. It was unheard of that anyone but the Provincial Council would select a Sister Servant. Dr. Denney was so advised and in two days a new Sister Servant presented herself with her credentials. Sister Catherine was torn between an almost scrupulous loyalty to Superiors and the recognition that, under the new administration, only Sister Martha could handle this big governmental job with the professional know-how that it required. But, the new Sister Servant was already in the Community Room, and she had to welcome her. In her heart she felt a great foreboding, but, when she saw who the new Sister Servant was, she all but fainted—it was none other than her beloved Sister Stella Lacey.

7

Dr. Denney, in time, became one of the best friends the Community had. But he was young at this period, and it was his first time in a leadership position. His reaction—it seemed cold at the time—was to treat Sister

Stella as a guest of the Sisters. This meant he saw no reason to interview her or to show any other sign of acceptance. To this day, guests of the personnel (including the Sisters' visitors) pay their own room and board for the duration of their stay, so this was no particular slight aimed at Sister Stella; but she felt it to be a great humiliation at the time.

The Sisters all suffered at this major squall, but none more so than Sister Catherine and Sister Martha. They knew the rules of the game and understood Dr. Denney's position; but both of them felt he could deal more gently, both with Sister Stella and with Superiors in St. Louis. He had spoken; he would not retreat or retract any of his pronouncements.

Even so, his conscience must have bothered him. He did not like to hurt the feelings of the Sisters. He knew that Carville was remarkable for the union of hearts and minds, with no petty jealousies; and always the patients' needs came first. What if the Commanding Officer in St. Louis should withdraw the Sisters? He probably mentioned this fear to Sister Martha. Of course, this is all a matter of conjecture, but, if he spoke to Sister Martha, she would be quick to tell him that the Commanding Officer in St. Louis would be within her rights if she did. At any rate, getting back to visible facts, he sent another letter to St. Louis.

He offered this compromise: he said that the office of Chief Dietitian was at the same level of command and prestige as that of chief nurse. The duty consisted of hiring and firing kitchen personnel, filling the office of purchasing agent, keeping accounts, making out records and sending them to Washington, evaluating food expenditures, and the services of the various personnel, recommending promotions, etc. It was an exacting position and the under-officer who was filling the position was unsatisfactory. In Dr. Denney's opinion, this would be a better job for combining with the duty of Sister Servant, and he suggested that Sister Catherine would be acceptable.

Sister Catherine knew nothing of this. If she had, her sleep would be more troubled than it had been for the last two months, because she would recognize that the Commanding Officer of Carville was again mixing in the affairs of the Commanding Officer in St. Louis. Meanwhile the morale of the Sisters was greatly lowered. Sister Catherine had no way of knowing how she stood with her long loved friend, Sister Stella Lacey. Sister Stella could hardly be blamed if she felt that Sister Catherine and Sister Martha could have eased the situation, because they both had such influence with Dr. Denney. But Sister Stella had never worked in a government hospital.

In due time, Sister Catherine received a letter from Sister Eugenia, telling her of Doctor Denney's suggestion. Although it was a kind letter, it, too, seemed to convey a little doubt and suspicion of collusion, for Sister Eugenia asked Sister Catherine if she thought anyone had been "influencing" her. She answered Sister Eugenia's letter promptly, pointing out how much further Sister Stella would be hurt by this appointment; that she herself had no qualifications for being Sister Servant. She asked to be spared this last straw to the threatened peace and harmony of the mission and said that she herself was about to collapse.

On August 12, 1923, Sister Catherine Sullivan was named Sister Servant of the United States Public

87

Health Hospital at Carville. Sister Stella Lacey was withdrawn; and Sister Catherine did collapse.

Anyone who has never had a *crise de nerfs* will never be quite able to understand the suffering entailed; nor the physical shock that follows in its wake. Shattered nerves render the body incapable of normal activity, for one can neither sleep nor eat, and the all enveloping weakness that results makes it impossible to walk or to engage in normal activities. Of course, people react in various ways, according to their own character and personality. With Sister Catherine it was an all encompassing apathy. Her mind was perfectly clear, but she could take no interest in what was going on about her. She wept a good deal at this time, and tears were unusual with her. She asked a Sister to write to Sister Eugenia and say that she was incapable of being a good Sister Servant and would she withdraw her from a situation that had become intolerable.

Whatever the Sister wrote, we shall never know. But a letter came by return mail from Sister Eugenia addressed to Sister Catherine. It said in part:

> I know that you are suffering, dear Sister, and you must not think that Sister Stella Lacey in any way holds you responsible. I know that this has affected you—but time has a way of healing wounds like these.

> What is of much greater concern to me is the state of your health. You have been under a great strain for many months, and perhaps some of it still lingers. Therefore, I want you to take bed-rest, until I feel you are able to be up and around again. When I say 'bed rest' I don't mean an afternoon nap. I want you to stay in bed, and remember it will take a long time. The chaplain will be glad to bring you Holy Communion

each morning. I shall send a carbon copy of this letter to Dr. Denney in the same mail as this.

Naturally this letter was a source of solace to Sister Catherine, but it worked no miracle for her health. She was very, very ill.

One day Doctor Denney came to visit her shortly after Sister Eugenia's letter. He said, "Say, I *like* that Sister Superior of yours. She's a great woman and I admire her very much. You must get well for her sake, as well as mine. By the way, before I came over from the office, I looked in your files to see how much time off you've had. I find that for seven years you've only had two weeks off for your annual retreats. That's a mere decimal point. You know what? Counting your no sick leaves and only half vacations, you have a backlog of ninety-three days. Isn't that fine?"

The Sisters at Carville are paid according to their rank in office. The higher the office, the higher the salary—with every day's absence docked. Poor Dr. Denney thought that it would cheer Sister Catherine to know that her illness would be without loss of pay. But at that time, nothing could cheer Sister Catherine except her spiritual life.

But time, good nursing care, and an understanding doctor, all acting under the watchful eye of Divine Providence, brought Sister, first out of her depression, then out of her weakness, and finally to robust health again. But as Sister Eugenia had warned her: "Remember it will take a long time."

It is a custom of the Community that in November or December 8 at the latest, each Sister Servant send in the annual report of her mission—the Sisters, their

89

duties, and her own stewardship. On November 28, 1923 Sister Catherine wrote her first report as Sister Servant of Carville. A brief excerpt gives insight into the depths of her humility; to the perceptive, the tell-tale evidence of deep suffering on the part of Sister Catherine, who could never bear anything that struck at the peace and harmony of the house in which she dwelt.

Excerpt from the Annual Report from Carville, dated November 28, 1923, and signed by Sister Catherine Sullivan:

> The loyalty to Superiors and devotion to this work shown by the Sisters of this mission during the trying times of the past year, lead me to hope that our Lord will reward their obedience by the appointment of a Sister Servant who can recompense them for their submission to the circumstances that placed me in this duty. With this ever present to me, I most humbly resign the duty of Sister Servant, and trust that my dear companions may reap in time, as they certainly will in eternity, the reward of their patience and fidelity.

Sister Eugenia must have been sincerely touched at this letter. Of course she did not relieve Sister Catherine of the office of Sister Servant. Not until 1936 did Sister Catherine leave Carville, and then it was to take up the office of Assistant Visitatrix.

SIX

To no one's amazement, Sister Catherine turned out to be a simply wonderful Sister Servant. There was perhaps a touch of over-orthodoxy in regard to the keeping of the Rules and Customs of the Community, but, to any who objected, she would point to the medical staff and their scrupulous adherence to any rules laid down (and there were many) by the government, many of which looked like red tape for the sake of red tape; and she would point up the instant obedience of the subordinate officers to any suggestion of the Commanding Officer. The Sisters would get the point—they had all had enough of the persistence of the C.O. of Carville.

1

Sister Laura Stricker, who is still serving in Carville, sends these notes about Sister Catherine as Sister Servant:

NOTES ON SISTER CATHERINE SULLIVAN

By Sister Laura

It was in February 1925 that I first met Sister Catherine Sullivan when I was missioned to Carville, Louisiana, where the United States Government has its National Leprosarium. Though only four and a half

91

years' vocation, this was my third mission and I thought I was a complete failure and thus I came to Carville with misgivings. I was under the impression that one had to be very special to work in a government hospital. When Sister Eugenia, then Visitatrix, asked if I had any fear about coming to Carville, I answered, "No, my only fear is that I will not measure up to the requirements of the government." Sister Catherine had a keen insight into human nature and she must have sensed my fears, for she did everything to make me feel at home. It did not take me long to realize that Sister Catherine was a woman of perfect charity and justice. She possessed an ingenious way of making friends with those who seemed discouraged or misunderstood.

I had the privilege of being prepared for my First Holy Vows by Sister Catherine. Sister could not tolerate failings against charity or even a critical remark about anyone, and severely reproved any uncharitable remarks. In 1925, the morning rising was at four o'clock and I simply could not keep my eyes open at meditation. She insisted I make the effort to keep awake by standing up a number of times and, if I was still sleepy, to leave the chapel and wash my face in an effort to waken myself. She advised me to prepare for the meditation the evening previous and to write down a thought on which I could meditate the following morning. She would follow up my efforts and wait for me after breakfast to ascertain if I had taken a resolution and an ejaculatory prayer to be said frequently during the day. If I failed to do so, she required me to return to the chapel, read the meditation and report to her. Many times, seeing that I could not get a thought to apply to myself, she would suggest a resolution and an ejaculatory prayer.

Sister was far ahead of her times in the matter of

education. There were several of the Sisters at Carville who had not completed their high school education, so she engaged the most competent teachers from our "St. Vincent Institute: A Select School for Young Ladies" (just 14 miles from Carville, and across the Mississippi River). They came every weekend and we were in class all day. Then they came for the entire summer and we had classes all day long. Other Sisters, who had finished their high school, took laboratory courses in physiotherapy and occupational therapy. Sister Teresa Kelly and I studied pharmacy and, after taking (and passing) our State Boards, received our certificates authorizing us to practice pharmacy in the State of Louisiana.

Sister also sent me to Louisiana State for my Bachelor in Music, so that I could become Social Director for the patients. We had a very active department: drama, play-acting, chorale, and all the trimmings. Once, when Sister heard they were offering a course at L.S.U. in Catholic Church Music, she sent me to take the course so that the patients could sing Gregorian Masses as well as the kind of operatic Masses from Mozart, Rosenbaum, etc., so popular in that day.

Sister also tried to bring higher education to the patients. She would import the best professors from L.S.U. and elsewhere to lecture on every subject under the sun.

Sister was responsible for the building of the beautiful Sacred Heart Chapel of Romanesque architecture, with its beautiful liturgical marble altar and mahogany reredos and life-size crucifix. To this end Sister wrote articles for the *Catholic Church Extension Magazine* and most of the funds were donated by the Extension Society.

While Sister Catherine was in Carville, she did not confine her apostolate to this area, but carried on correspondence with young girls who were attracted to the works at Carville and thus brought vocations to our Community. Thus the work of her last years in Community of being the Director of the Daughters of Charity Information Service had its beginnings in Carville.

Sister Catherine gave me a great surprise one year when I was named to make the Indianapolis retreat. Unknown to me, she had written to my parents and to my two sisters, who are Sisters of Providence, inviting them to Indianapolis and providing them with financial aid to do so in order that we might have a family reunion. I had not seen my sisters since they entered their community. What a surprise when I came out of retreat and found my family there!

Sister never mistrusted one and never believed another's report, but waited to hear the story from the other one in question. I trusted her implicity and told her my faults even though I knew she would be stern with me; but I remembered that she would also be understanding.

Sister always frowned on a statement prefixed by the words "It's too bad that so and so. . ." She regarded every event as God's Will. When we would say: "It's a blessing she died," (referring to a suffering patient) Sister would say, "Don't say *that* when *I* die!"

Though Sister was strict about regularity at spiritual exercises, she advised many times: "If a patient wants to talk to you in order to get his troubles aired, stay and let the patient talk, even if you are late." But, if it became a habit, she required regularity.

Sister Catherine meant so much to me in my early years of imprudence and helped me over many a temptation to discouragement.

Sister Laura has summarized magnificently some of Sister Catherine's best and most appreciated qualities. These were qualities that affected the entire Community in light of future events when Sister would hold the two highest offices in the province—those of Province-Superior and Assistant Visitatrix.

Everyone appreciated her remarkable sense of justice. She froze at the introductory words to a juicy bit of gossip. "They say—" she would interrupt with, "Who's *they*, Sister? Anybody we know?" As Sister Laura says, she would never listen to one side of a story about another. In her frequent advices to the Sisters later, both as Assistant and as Visitatrix, she would speak of detraction as if it were some kind of reptile; and she would urge upon us this principle: "Although an angel be the accuser, Sisters, I implore you, refuse to believe the story. Nobody but God Himself can know the heart of the accused. Judge not and you yourself will not be judged."

2

Meantime, back at Carville. Sister Martha was proving to be a providential choice for Chief Nurse. Her duty forced her to be more outgoing. She taught the Sister Nurses new techniques, and, at long last, she allowed herself to love. Sister Catherine's example could not fail to impress her; her lovableness was irresistible. The laboratory work being done by Sister Hilary Ross fascinated her and a common bond grew between them to the point where Sister Hilary nicknamed Sister Martha "Brother," and Sister Martha responded in turn, so that all the Sisters had an example of brotherly love before them. No one could ever, in her wildest imagination, conceive of Sister Martha as a "big Sister," but "Brother" was credible. This gives us insight into the unity and harmony that reigned in the house (which is what the Daughters call their "convents" everywhere).

Dr. Denney, as the years wore on, was proud as a peacock of his star-studded staff and did not find it necessary to lean upon his office as Commanding Officer. He gave wide authority for the "time out" that was necessary for crossing the river to Baton Rouge several times a week, and was proud of the Sisters' intellectual achievement.

3

Speaking of intellectual achievement, it was hard to come by, for in those times (1923) the Community was sending only school Sisters on for higher studies, because there, in the school field, was where the pressure was. Speaking of these times, Sister Catherine once said: "I was very anxious to send any of the Sisters who had finished high school to Louisiana State University. As this (in my mind) meant an on-going thing, I asked Sister Visitatrix for a general permission. I painted in roseate terms how easy of access (over the river and through the woods) the University would be, and Dr. Denney had approved wholeheartedly, because (I added this part ominously) he predicted that it will be no time at all before nurses will be required to earn the Bachelor degree in their field, so Dr. Denney thinks this is great foresight on our part." Sister Eugenia must have acted immediately, without consulting her councillors. She wired: "Permission granted." Taking no chances with fate's antic ways and with a sense of foreboding, Sister hurried to act on the permission. She drove to the University and registered Sister Hilary for courses leading to a Bachelor of Science with a major in chemistry.

Awaiting Sister Catherine's return to Carville, from Baton Rouge, was a telegram. It read:

Disregard permission granted. Letter follows.

Sister Eugenia

Sister Catherine lost no time in getting to a typewriter. She would have to get a letter to St. Louis before any "letter followed" . . . She wrote that she had accepted Sister at her word and registered Sister Hilary promptly, as time was short. She had also paid tuition in advance. How could she now cancel plans? It was sure to begin a round of correspondence with Dr. Denney.

Sister Eugenia telegraphed her approval, and thus Sister Hilary Ross became a famed pathologist, with international prestige. She was asked to read papers in various countries at international conventions. An interesting sidelight on Sister Hilary and the influence of attending international conventions (how far a little candle throws its beam!) is that after her retirement from Carville, when she was really past the age limit, she volunteered for a foreign mission, and—this sounds incredible—she was assigned to Japan. She works in the dispensary there and—as we see her on her visits to St. Louis, and to her relatives—we all say that she is incurably Japanese.

Meanwhile, Sister Catherine always had a backlog of invitations to speak in all parts of the country. Hansen's disease could be a morbid theme for an entertaining talk. Womens' Clubs wanted to learn all they could about this—at that time fairly unknown disease—and saw its fascinating possibilities for small talk across bridge tables; for the more serious-minded, it became a bond of interest toward which various charitable activities might be directed. Sister Catherine was a perceptive psychologist. She suited her talks to her audience. But, even when she was speaking to the medical profession, she knew how to insert little asides and amusing anecdotes. If this biography were to fail in showing both humor and pathos as facets of Sister Catherine's personality, it would have failed, at least partially, in its purpose to present Sister Catherine as she was. Of the many anecdotes that might be recorded, space allows for only a few.

Once she was speaking to a large audience of Vincentian Priests and Seminarians:

> It was July 19, feast of St. Vincent de Paul. As dietitian, I was running back and forth between kitchen and the Sisters' refectory, both of which were separate from the patients' culinary department. Naturally, I wanted a special menu to celebrate the event—for the Sisters as well as the patients. This called for a conference with our chef.
>
> "Jason," I said, "do you know St. Vincent de Paul?"
>
> "Yassam, Sister, I knows him."
>
> "Well, we are having a big feast all day today in his honor. You know he really got the Daughters of Char-

ity organized to do good works all over the world. And just think of *this*, Jason, he has 46,000 Daughters!"

Jason shook his head in stark disbelief. "That ain't the same St. Vincent I knows. We got a statue to him up in our Church. He's a priest—he ain't got no children."

There was real pathos to some of her anecdotes which left not one dry eye in the audience:

At Christmas benefactors were very generous with the patients. But it was rather difficult to "surprise" them with anything. They had every material comfort that humanitarianism could provide. But this year a well known business man had contributed a check, allowing each a special-choice present—one that he could choose for himself. I took charge of visiting each patient to ask what, out of the whole world, he would choose for himself. The ceiling was five dollars per patient.

As I went the rounds, I came to the room of a dear little old woman with snow white hair. She was blind, had lost her sense of smell, and all sensation of touch. Only the sense of hearing remained. I sat down for my Christmas visit with her.

Taking her hand in mine, though I knew she could feel nothing, I said: "Annie, suppose you could have *anything* on earth for a Christmas present this year—just anything. What would you choose?"

It must have been on her mind, for, not taking time to think, she said, ever so gently: "Sister, I have no relatives left. I have no one but you. But, if you gave me a choice for a Christmas present, I would ask for a flowering plant."

"Really?" I asked, almost stunned at the request. "You won't be able to see it, you know; you won't be able to smell it, and you won't be able to touch it. Would you really like that better than a pretty shawl, or - - -?"

"Sister, I know that *I* won't be able to see it, except in my imagination; I know that I can't feel or smell it— except by make-believe. But Sister, when the other patients come in to visit on Christmas morning, like so many do, I can hear them say: 'Oh, what a beautiful plant! Where did you get such a lovely thing?'

"And I can smile and say with pride: 'A friend sent it'."

The following anecdote was told with tears in her own eyes. When she told it, however, she always modestly substituted the words "Daughters of Charity" for "Sister Catherine" which, however, is the true version:

I became very interested in a well-educated man to whom leprosy came like a bolt from the blue. He was a very successful business executive, happily married with several children of whom he was inordinately proud.

Like all patients he entered under an assumed name. His malady was far advanced before the right diagnosis was made. I don't know what arrangements he made with his wife to shield his children from ever knowing the truth about his illness; but one heart-breaking pledge he asked of her was to forget him and never attempt to see him; nor come to his funeral.

My special interest in him was that he professed to be an atheist. I was determined, with the help of God, to make a Christian of him.

I spent a half hour, and sometimes longer, with him each day. We would discuss current events, books, foreign affairs, and sports. I read widely on these topics so as to be ready for our far-ranging conversations.

We became very friendly, and the Sister in charge of the pavilion where he was located told me that he would watch the clock and if I were a bit late he would ask: "Isn't Sister Catherine coming today?" But I always came. He had made it plain from the first that he wanted no discussion of religion.

Finally, he became so ravaged with the disease that he had to be moved to what we would call today an intensive care unit. The day before he died, weak but very alert, he said to me:

"Sister, how can a woman of your amazing intelligence wear the same dress every day, and work like a slave in this place? Something is behind it—what is the motivation?"

"Love," I answered quickly.

"You mean a humanitarian love for the needy?" he asked.

"No," I said. "Love of a Person."

"Whom?" he insisted.

"God," I said.

"There's no such person, and I cannot understand a woman with your brains believing that."

I left him shortly, because I could see that he was becoming weaker and our conversation bothered him.

"Come again," he said, as I was leaving.

In the early morning hours of the next day I was summoned to him at his request. I hurriedly dressed and within a few moments was kneeling by his bed. I took his fingerless hand in both of mine, and as I did so he whispered hoarsely: "Sister, if only I could give you something for all you have done for me. What would please you . . . tell me quickly before I die."

"Frank," I said, "just four little words from you; just say, 'I believe in God.' That will make me exquisitely happy." I held my breath for his answer.

Two tears slid down his cheeks from beneath his eyelids. As I pressed his poor hand in hope, and in strangled prayer, for I was fighting for a soul, he opened his eyes, and looked directly into mine. In a weak voice that was trying urgently to be strong, he said his last words on earth:

"I believe in Sister Catherine."

SEVEN

It was a quiet Community joke, when, in 1926, Rome enforced Canon 505 which said that all local superiors would have to be changed every six years to another mission or released from her office of administration for at least one year. This meant for our Community quite an upheaval, since every Sister Servant would be uprooted from where she had been (Heaven knows how long); and it touched every private Sister because there would be the ordeal of having a new Sister Servant. So each one took a second look at the bird in the hand, and wondered what the bush would yield. But the quiet joke recalled even today in the Community was the coincidence that the first Sister Servant missioned under the new decree from Rome was a very tiny (quite capable) person whose full name was Sister Regina Gunn. "Canon 505—and off goes the littlest gun" became a household word for a long time. The constant missioning that went on for the whole year of 1926 was a nervous but humorous time as is the case with the Daughters of Charity everywhere who seem to have a special gift for injecting laughter when tears threaten.

1

Sister Catherine stood ready like a soldier for any summons that—however painful—would call her to another duty. The days became edgier, and nerves were

103

taut; but the knowledge that one is doing or assenting to God's Will makes intelligent obedience synonomous with a deep-seated peace of soul. Sister Martha especially had need of summoning all of her soldierly strength to meet this trial.

But, strangely enough, there was no trial; no sorrow of separation. The Sisters had simply forgotten that God's eye is always on the sparrow, and He, quite visibly was their real and only Commanding Officer.

Sister Eugenia wrote that the work of Carville came under the category of "Special Cases" (which meant special treatment) and that Rome had approved a double new term for Sister Catherine as Superior. She had been Sister Servant for thirteen years, out of the twenty-one years she had spent in Carville.

2

On an afternoon in 1936, she was seated in her office when she saw Sister Martha walking, as if in pain, down that part of the "mile" that leads to the Sisters' Quarters. Thinking to meet Sister halfway, Sister Catherine started out, but noticed that Sister Martha had turned into the Sacred Heart Chapel where she stayed a full hour. Not wishing to intrude on a conversation with God, Sister Catherine went back to the office and waited.

Finally Sister Martha came to Sister Catherine and said: "Sister, I am having serious abdominal pain." She looked earnestly at Sister Catherine and said in a tired but convincing voice: "I am dying, Sister." Sister Catherine hurriedly called an ambulance and rode with Sister Martha to New Orleans' Hotel Dieu (hospital) where our Sisters awaited her arrival. The next morning Sister Martha Lawlor died.

We pass over the mourning at Carville, where Sister Martha was so much loved by staff and patients alike. Sister Catherine accepted this as God's Will, but could not understand that He had given her no premonition that this was to happen, as He so often did. But of one thing she was absolutely certain: with Sister Martha safely in Heaven with a God who understands us all, because He made us, she herself was now on His agenda for change.

3

In 1930, Sister Caroline Collins, one of the most beloved Sister Servants in the province, was named Assistant Visitatrix. Now at that time the position of the Assistant Visitatrix was pretty much like that of the Vice President of the United States, a sort of stand-by job that occasionally merited half a column on the fourth page of the newspapers. She missed acutely her work as Principal of St. Patrick Grade and High School, Chicago. Her Sisters felt as though the world had stopped when she bade them goodby. Of course, they would meet her frequently at retreats in St. Louis, but that was not like having her for their very own Sister Servant.

How this happens to be recorded in Sister Catherine's biography is that the custom of the Community is to have newly-made Provincial Superiors make an eight day retreat at the Motherhouse in Paris, then a two or three month period of travel, always beginning with Rome.

Very shortly after Sister Caroline's arrival in St. Louis, she was notified of her European Tour and was told that Sister Catherine Sullivan would be her companion. The two of them had a wonderful time, free as birds, with the chief attraction for a Collins and a Sullivan, the green hills of Ireland. If space permitted, their letters home would make a rich contribution to this biography—but it would also take space that cannot be afforded when one is trying to compress a very active life of eighty-two years into a possible 200 pages.

Sister Caroline was a faithful and loving support to Sister Eugenia who was herself almost too old now for active duty. She had sent in her resignation two or three times, but Superiors at Paris told her she must carry the cross to the end. Sister Eugenia died July 11, 1936, and Sister Caroline was named her successor and—unknown to happen before—the new Assistant Visitatrix was named in the same letter . . . none other than Sister Catherine Sullivan.

4

Writing to a very dear friend in England, Sister Mary Meehan, with whom she regularly corresponded, Sister Catherine describes her always unusual reactions to great events. Here are a few excerpts from her letters written while Sister was still "in shock" over the news from St. Louis:

> Isn't it incredible? Or rather, are not both things incredible? First, that I should be preparing to leave Carville; and secondly, that I should be preparing to leave it for the duty of Assistant? I know that you have heard of the change, because I received a letter from Sister Catherine Croucher some days ago.

Everything (for Carville has been everything to me for more than twenty years) came to an end just as quickly and decisively and as unexpectedly as death. On September 28, Sister Zoe* and I returned from Baton Rouge at 4 P.M. after a pleasant afternoon's shopping. As soon as we reached home, I sat down in the office to answer a delightful letter received that morning from Archbishop Rummel. At 4:15 a telegram arrived: "Important message awaits you at Marillac Seminary. Please come to St. Louis without delay. You will return to Carville after conference."

My dear, I know now exactly the calmness which supervenes when a sacrifice is inevitable. I glanced at the clock; if I could leave in an hour, I could drive down to New Orleans and get an evening train. I showed the telegram to Sister Zoe; asked her if she could get me packed up; knelt in the chapel and told our Lord that twenty years of perfect happiness was more than anyone was entitled to—and was on my way before I could get word to half of the Sisters, since most of them do not come up from the Colony until 5:30.

Of course, I hoped against hope. And at night, finding sleep rather out of the question, even on the most comfortable of Pullman's, do you know what I did? Said our chaplet? Guess again. Prayed to our holy founders? No. I just kept my mind fixed on what I would order for breakfast! Yes, it seemed to me that in a world that had suddenly gone chaotic, I could bring order back and restore normalcy by planning a meal, and stopping life just at the point where an obsequious waiter says: "More cream in your coffee, ma'am?" Well, when I got into Union Station at 4 P.M. the next day and saw Sister Caroline, Assistant, and

---

*The same Sister Zoe who had played checkers in Alton, Illinois, with young Sister Catherine.

Sister Isabella, Treasurer, at the station, my heart sank; I knew very well *they* had not come down to check a trunk!

And oh, how merrily (?) we chatted on the way to Marillac. All about the war in Spain and the condition of the crops and the coming Presidential election - - - but not a word as to why I was there. The Habit Sisters and Seminary Sisters were lined up at the front door, but I was too dazed to take in what it meant.

But the Reverend Director was also waiting in due state in his office, and it was he who handed me the patent, letters, etc. I learned later that the circular of the Superior General, Father Souvay, announcing Sister Caroline's appointment as Visitatrix and mine as Assistant had been read at 2 P.M. the day before. All I could think was that our dear Lord had liberally sugar-coated the pill, because we were all so happy to have Sister Caroline for Visitatrix that it did not matter at all who the Assistant would be.

Promptly the next day (like something that has been sent for on approval and did not suit), I was sent back to Carville to make the Community's peace with the Government officials, the patients and the Sisters. Dr. Hazzeltine, the Commanding Officer (Dr. Denney had retired a few years ago), took the change like a soldier and a gentleman, stipulating only that I was to remain long enough to initiate my successor. So that accounts for my being still at Carville.

So far, my successor has not been named. The Sister Servant's position here is a very delicate one. De jure, she does not exist; but de facto she figures rather largely in the picture. Officially, all of the nursing affairs are referred to the Chief Nurse. As long as the Chief Nurse and the Sister Servant are one, and a fine rapport exists with the Commanding Officer, all goes well.

I hasten to say that I know that all will continue to go well, but I feel I am much like a woman selecting a daughter-in-law when it comes to picking out someone for Carville. All of those comely and capable, efficient and virtuous Sister Servants, whom I have admired so much, suddenly develop flaws never seen before!

I think you will sense, dear Sister Mary, that if I speak lightly of leaving a labor loved for so long, it is simply because I dare not do otherwise until I have closed the books and written finis to a chapter which I had hoped to end with my life. If the Community had decided that someone else would do better here—oh, how readily would I have agreed. If the Government had found fault with my services, I would have been comforted by the thought of One "Who came unto His own and His own received Him not."

In my heart of hearts, I have always dreamed of something of the sort—years from now—and I would have looked upon that as the seal of the Master's approval of my work. But to have the burden of what the Community and the Government look upon as an honor, thrust upon me at the same time that I must face the pain of separation from Carville—dear Sister Mary, I fear I must have great spiritual pride for it all seems to me to be so common-place.

In humble imitation of Paul who knew "nothing but Jesus Christ and Him crucified," for this long while I have known nothing but the Master, suffering, despised, rejected and misunderstood in the person of our patients. Known Him and loved Him with a joy that made each day a marvel of new joy. Is that an adequate preparation for the new duty?

Even as I say that, some lines and sentences from that inspired work, *The Anchorhold,* recur to me. "She

standeth so very near to the cross, and she standeth so
very still, that she sees things from God's point of
view." Truly, I have been privileged to stand very near
indeed to the cross of the suffering poor. And again,
as I look out at the high levees which have formed the
limits of my duty and my desires, I recall: "And between encompassing walls she hath found the infinite:
infinite pity, infinite understanding, infinite love."

5

After a few weeks in St. Louis, she writes again to
Sister Mary Meehan:

While we are speaking of geographical limits, do not
forget that Perryville, Missouri, where Sister Bertrande
is, is just eighty miles from here. Sister has found it
convenient to spend two weekends here since my arrival. Which rather bears out what my little stenog-
rapher in Carville said when I was missioned: "Well,
I know one person who will be glad—Sister Bertrande."

In regard to leaving Carville, dear Sister Mary, God
treated me, as He has always done, indulgently. Happy
as I was there; dearly as I loved the Sisters; eager as
I was to spend the rest of my life in the service of the
patients—when all that no longer spelled the Will of
God for me, I closed it as easily as I would a book that
I had finished.

And now I wait, with the contentment of a child, to
see what God wants me to do. At present, I am not
very much occupied, and certainly I keenly miss slip-
ping into a white hospital gown at 7 A.M., realizing
that I was putting on an armour, and would go forth
to battle, not only with disease, but with the more in-
sidious and deadly foes of rebellion, cynicism, bitter-

ness and despair. I never realized how intense the life was until I viewed it in perspective. I realize, though, that most of my work was "made" work—things entirely outside the regular line of duty. And I rather think it will not be long before I shall be "making" some work for myself here.

During the month in which I have occupied the Assistant's office, I have managed to give to it (with surprisingly little effort) a general air of untidiness and disorder hitherto foreign to the Marillac, but which is very familiar to me.

I have for my Secretary a charming little Sister named Sister Emily. She made her appearance in the office a few days after my arrival and asked, in a perfectly correct tone to go with the perfectly correct office, if there was anything I would like her to do. I sensed there was a crisis, for at that moment my soul was longing for the glad disarray, not to say actual chaos, of Carville ways and days. I sat a bit straighter in the chair; with a meditative finger I moved a paper weight back to the exact spot where it has rested for twenty years and then replied: "Yes, Sister, if you please, I would like to dictate a few letters."

Now, while the letters were semi-official, they were to Sisters whom I had known—lo, these many years. So, right in the middle of a perfectly conservative sentence—I went radical. Sister Emily paused, looked up rather panic-stricken, caught my eye, and—well, her name is not O'Flaherty for nothing. Since then she appears hopefully twice a day, gaily asking: "Any letters, Sister?" The Sisters are very good to me, Sister Mary, and I cannot begin to tell you how grateful I am.

As to Sister Catherine's seemingly unconquerable fault of untidiness, a little anecdote, which points up a singular, almost miraculous growth in will power, should be told here.

Shortly after Sister Catherine became Assistant Visitatrix, she remarked quite happily to a Sister friend, a very close friend, that she was just about the untidiest woman in the world and maybe should be given an award. The Sister replied that she would like to give the award, if Sister would accept it as an act of love. Sister Catherine sobered. "Something's coming up. Yes, I shall accept it as another of your countless proofs of love."

Thus assured, the friend said gently: "Sister, once, say at Carville, you represented yourself. Just you. And we all loved you just because you *are* you. But now you represent the whole province. Think of that in relation to untidiness, will you, Sister? The one exception is your desk, because anyone can see that within that disorder is a certain order all your own—and it works out just fine." Sister Catherine impulsively kissed the Sister and said: "Thank you, angel. I never doubted your love and now I never shall."

The point of this anecdote is that the subject never came up again. Never could anyone impute untidiness to Sister Catherine again and they never did. She was without any affectation (she was incapable of that), always well-groomed, and her room was as austerely neat as if it were kept as a guest room. She (gratefully?) accepted the reprieve about her desk, but it was *only* the desk. The rest of her office was never in the smallest disarray. Never once could anyone call her "untidy" again; and the friend lived under the same roof with her for more than thirty years.

6

Under date of September 25, Sister Catherine again writes to Sister Mary Meehan in England:

I am aghast! I have read the first paragraph of your letter which ends with the sentence: "You have not written this year." That hardly seems possible; I am very sure I wrote sometime round the Easter season. But, in any case, I'll take my clue from that and run over some of my activities for this year.

Sister Caroline is very generously determined that I shall get well acquainted with the Province, so the Marillac Sisters have taken to saying pleasantly that I come home only to have my washing done. Early in the year, I made a trip to the houses in my native state of Texas, timing my arrival at Sherman to coincide with the golden jubilee of a dear ancient Sister there. You may recall that Sister Teresa Kelly, who spent ten years with us at Carville, is Sister Servant there. She very naively remarked that for once she was glad to be a Sister Servant, because that gave her a greater claim to the Assistant's time.

I had been home just a few days when the serious illness of two Sister Servants in Chicago, Illinois, left the Infant Home and the Hospital with no one to direct them. They are both very important establishments with a large corps of Sisters. I spent two months there, dividing my time between the two houses. Now, if you get a map and look up Missouri, you will also find Kansas City and St. Joseph (These cities are only an hour's distance apart). In Kansas City, I, for the first time, found out how a Boys' Home is conducted and dived into the history of our Kansas City Boys' Home. A Visitation at Keokuk, Iowa, was sandwiched somewhere in the months. And now I have just come back from a flying trip to Louisiana and Texas during which I had the joy of spending a day and a half at Carville.

Joy? No, not that entirely. As a matter of fact, I experienced even more pain at parting this time. But I hasten to say that's perfectly all right, and, if our dear Lord allowed the flames which I thought just flickering out to brighten up again, He will know how to smother them in time.

Since most of Sister Catherine's work as Assistant Visitatrix was strictly Community (and in those days "strictly Community" was "hush-hush"; now it is, happily, everybody's business and "news" letters from the Visitatrix come out weekly for all to read and "speculate" upon—sometimes noisily), we are grateful for Sister Catherine's letters in which she can speak for herself. We quote from Sister Mary Meehan's letters because they extend over a period of thirty-nine years. The following tells of our taking over a second Charity Hospital in Louisiana:

I know I have not written you this year so I shall just take a glance over the calendar and pick up the high lights. Perhaps dearest to our Lord was our acceptance of a new hospital in Lafayette, Louisiana—a State institution of two hundred and fifty beds, exclusively for the poor. Bishop Jeanmard of that diocese is a personal friend of our good Father Souvay who has relatives in Lafayette.

Consequently, despite the fewness of our vocations, we could not refuse this institution when the Superior General signified his desire of our acceptance. Of course, we ourselves were only too eager to take up a work so decidedly ours.

I made several trips South in the interests of this project, but was not present for the opening. I do wish I had a copy of the circular letter which Bishop Jeanmard sent to the priests of his diocese asking them to be present for the opening of the hospital and to thank God for the blessings that would come with the Sisters' presence. Truly, our Holy Founder, St. Vincent, must have smiled most heartily at what was an echo of his own day.

One notices here—if one is perceptive—how Sister Catherine's work with the state and federal government in Carville had given her a wide range of experience that was tremendously useful to the Community.

7

In 1947 Sister Catherine writes:

Who would have thought, when I sent you the card from Emmitsburg, with the notation that you would hear from me soon, that the "soon" would prolong itself to more than a month. Well, dear Sister Mary, letters or no letters, you know that you are always in my heart.

Let's see—I did tell you on that card that I had been traveling for two months. Traveling that took me to Chicago and Milwaukee—the most northern part of our province—to Carville and New Orleans—the most southern parts; and then on to the Eastern province, where I spent some time in Washington, D.C., Emmitsburg, and Baltimore.

The business that detained me for quite some time in Chicago was installing Sister Bertrande Meyers as Sister Servant at Catholic Social Center, which will, in a few months, be replaced by Marillac House in another part of the city. Of course you remember my speaking frequently of Sister Bertrande. Since earning her doctorate, she has been Superintendent of Schools and Educational Directress. You may well believe that we have made some sacrifice in now turning her abilities and talents into the channel of social works; but those works are, above all others, for the Poor, so why should anything be preferred to them?

Anyway, Sister Bertrande, with her unlimited energy and her genius for organization, will keep her fingers on the pulse of the schools, and continue to direct the Sisters' studies at the various universities. I shall enclose some clippings about Marillac House (its corporate title is Marillac Social Center, but Marillac House is the popular name) and you will hear much more of it from time to time.

Now for the business that took me, first to Carville, and then to Washington. I was invited, by the Surgeon General of the United States Public Health Service, to be a member of the National Advisory Board on Leprosy. The Surgeon General has only three National Advisory Boards—one on Cancer, one on Mental Health, and now, this latest, on Leprosy. It shows how much attention they are paying to the disease that has been, for too many centuries, ignored. May I say, modestly, that the Advisory Boards are made up of experts in their particular fields—and that, of the sixteen members on the Leprosy Advisory Board, I am the lone lorn woman?

We met in Washington at the Public Health Service Headquarters, and I think we really made history. Practically, we wrote an Emancipation Proclamation for patients with leprosy. It was decided to establish clinics in all the large cities, in connection with the Marine Hospitals which are dotted all over the United States. As each case of leprosy is diagnosed, it will be

116

considered individually, and no longer will blanket segregation apply. Many of the patients need not be removed from their homes nor even from their business or employment; they can continue to lead normal lives and get the treatment they need at special clinics.

Of course, side-by-side with this new approach to the disease must go a campaign of education for the public—beginning with doctors and nurses, who, as a rule, know as little about leprosy as does the ordinary layman. That, too, was all mapped out. If I can find them, I'll also enclose some clippings on that subject.

Sunshine and shadows mingle in life. While we were yet in the glow of satisfaction caused by the accomplishments of the Advisory Committee, we were shocked by news from Carville that one of the patients went berserk and made a murderous attack on Sister Mary Meade, attempting to cut her throat. The man, who has been there some six or seven years, was always rated as "queer," but no one dreamed that he had homicidal tendencies.

One Sunday morning (January) Sister Mary Meade was in the diet kitchen, getting things ready for the patients' dinner, when this man came in and made some very unreasonable demand. Without even turning from what she was doing, Sister said: "Now, Mac, you see that I am busy. Go back to your room and I'll talk to you later." The man immediately advanced on her with his pocket knife, slashing her throat before the screams of a girl nearby caused Sister Georgiana to run into the room.

Though Sister Georgiana is just a mite of a thing, she grabbed the man's arm and prevented further harm and the patient was finally subdued. Sister Mary Meade walked down a short flight of stairs, and, with

117

blood pouring from the gaping wound, collapsed at the Sister Servant's feet. You can imagine the shock. However, Providence permitted that a number of the Sisters, and also a doctor, were there to give first aid; and, after that, Sister was taken in an ambulance to Hotel Dieu, New Orleans, where she is recovering nicely. Her collar, which was cut through, deflected the knife somewhat, so that most of the wound was lateral, rather than transverse.

The patients feel as shocked as the Sisters, for during her twenty-six years at Carville, Sister Mary Meade has been the personification of devotedness. Even though the man was adjudged violently insane, they feel terrible that a thing like that should have been done by one of the patients. However, you and I know, Sister Mary, that Daughters of Charity can take those things "in stride"; and, in fact, Sister Mary Meade is only waiting, with not too great patience, until she can be discharged from Hotel Dieu to go back to Carville and take up her work again.

Once when Sister Catherine was asked if there was much violence at the leprosarium she said, her dimples showing, "Not really often, Sister. Just occasional excitement; for example, I remember one day at my morning meditation hearing the unmistakable sound of a revolver shot. I tore out of the Chapel and found that a hundred yards from me a man lay on the ground, gasping his last breath. A man was standing over him with a smoking gun. Chester, the man with the revolver, scratched his head, looked at me in a sort of bewildered manner and said: 'Sistah, don't things happen funny? I was standing here talking to Leo and suddenly he became shot.' Just as we have our own Post Office, we have our own jail."

118

On trains and planes, and on her brief intervals at Marillac during these busy times, Sister Catherine read avidly in all the fields covered by our varied apostolate here in the United States. She became an "expert" on Children's Institutions—not an armchair expert—for after having read much on the subject of Children's Institutions, just for one example, she spent weeks at the Homes we have dotted across the country, thus getting first-hand experience working with the group leaders and other members of the Staff. Most eagerly of all, she was interested in how philosophies of administration worked in various states and regions. They had changed much since her days at St. Rose's.

She likewise attended conventions, where she was so vocal "from the floor" that everybody got to know Sister Catherine and her advanced views in child care. They clamored to have her on committees, commissions, podiums, and finally on the Governing Boards. She was invited to speak at all important conventions and came to exert great influence on The National Conference of Catholic Charities, writing for them various handbooks that she knew would be helpful to the Sisters engaged in apostolic work in the field of Social Welfare.

She was responsible, under the leadership of Father Slattery of the St. Louis Archdiocesan Catholic Charities, for the amazingly successful Child Guidance Clinic (a service to "bright" but emotionally disturbed children of all races, color and creed, but under Catholic auspices, of course). In a letter to Sister Mary Meehan, she tells of its beginning:

On Sunday last we had our first meeting of the Board of Directors of the Child Center of Our Lady of Grace. That is the title we have given to our Child Guidance Clinic—isn't it beautifully suggestive of what we will need to make our dealings with the little ones successful?

We invited thirty-eight prominent men and women of St. Louis to act on the Board of Directors, and, wonder of wonders, received not one refusal! We had intended limiting the Board to twenty-five, but, when all accepted, what could we do but expand the number?

This is the third Child Guidance Clinic to be started in St. Louis; the other two, one a Municipal Clinic, and one attached to a secular University, were each discontinued after some years—frankly, they were failures. We will not fail, please God, because we have what the others did not and could not have—a Catholic philosophy. This Child Center will figure largely in my letters from now on, I am sure.

Sister Catherine had a wonderful way of listening to the various private Sisters tell of their spurts of inspiration. She looked upon every Sister as an "idea woman," and in that way she acted as a talent scout for our different works.

One Sister, Dolores Girault, who was Mexican by birth and entered with an extra fine family background and experience in Mexican culture, had always an almost obsessive occupation for bettering the living standards of the lower class Mexicans in the United States. Sister Catherine was most interested in her ideas for a maternity unit separate from the general hospital, Hotel Dieu, that we operate in El Paso, Texas. Again we can "hear it like it was" from Sister Catherine's unfailing pen to Sister Mary:

120

As you can see, I am once more in my beloved El Paso. You will recall that I spent some weeks out here last June, consulting with the Catholic Welfare Association in regard to maternity care for the poor mothers of El Paso—of whom there are thousands among the Mexican population, who have had to resort to non-Catholic agencies for help.

We planned a pre and post-natal Clinic and a maternity unit, the latter to be on the hospital grounds, the former six blocks away. They set to work with a will, and at their invitation I returned to El Paso on the Feast of Saint Patrick, to accept, in the name of the Community, the maternity building, which would be opened on the Feast of Saint Joseph—appropriately enough, since it is named "St. Joseph's." And oh, Sister Mary, it is a perfect little jewel of a building. For once, the poor have the very best of everything, in planning, in building and in equipping it. It is, as I told the gentlemen, an act of Catholic faith as well as of Catholic charity. For Catholic faith, taking literally the words of our Lord, "Whatsoever you do unto the least of Mine, that you do unto Me," would offer to Christ in the Poor only the best that it has. The Clinic is also complete in every detail.

Now, my plan was to remain here two or three days, then go to Carville by way of New Orleans. (A thirty-six hours straight trip, by the way.) But these excellent Catholic people, having tasted success in one project, are eager to go on to more. So, what we have planned, and actually started, in less than a week—well, one week, to be exact—reads like a fairy tale.

However, let me give you the setting, first. Mr. Joseph Morgan, a large, general contractor, the wealthiest citizen and most influential Catholic in El Paso, has been for months a patient in the hospital with inoperable cancer. However, his mind is keen and he is able to be up in his room and even down to his office almost every day. Also, his four fine sons, whom he has trained in his views and ways, are all in his business and ready to carry out every suggestion of his.

Then (mark the uniquely providential situation) the recently appointed auxiliary Bishop, the active head of the diocese, has his living quarters at our hospital. So, one has but to plan in the morning, secure financial backing at noon, ecclesiastical approval in the evening, and lo, the thing is done.

On the twentieth, Mr. Morgan began to talk to me about a Community Center for the underprivileged (the now current term for the Poor) in connection with the San Jose Maternity Clinic. In this Center would be washing machines, where the poor mothers could bring the family washing to do; sewing machines that they could use; and in another section, a stove, refrigerators, etc., etc. where they would be taught cooking, with emphasis on children's foods and infant formulae. And, not the least important, there would also be rows of "community" showers; there the clients could enjoy the luxury of a bath.

After a lengthy discussion, Mr. Morgan said suddenly: "Well, draw your plans, Sister, and we'll start the building Monday." (And this was Thursday!) You may be sure Sister Dolores and I lost no time in doing so, and, when we took him the sketch, he immediately sent it down to his office to have a blueprint made.

Then I began to think that the mothers must of necessity bring a number of little ones with them, which would necessitate a playground. So on Sunday, Mr. Morgan, Bishop Metzger, Sister Dolores and I went down to look at a lot next to the yesterday-planned building. The outcome was that we decided to buy not only that lot for a playground, but two more as well. There is a house on each of the last two lots on which our covetous glance rested; one can be used for a Boys' Club—for the roughs and toughs and morons, excluded, by reason of moral or mental defects, from the Boy Scouts and kindred organizations here—and the other as a demonstration home for the School for Maids, which came mentally into existence as we looked at the house.

These poor Mexican girls must, for the most part, go into domestic service; but, coming from such hovels as they do, they are the despair of the women who hire them. We plan to give them a several months' course in those tasks which the ordinary home requires, including the use of electrical appliances. When we have them trained, we will conduct an employment agency, and can ask for the girls a better salary than they would dare ask for themselves.

If I do not dwell on how all this material assistance will be the means of aiding them spiritually, it is because you will obviously grasp that. The Ladies of Charity will help in the supervision of all this work, and I think that some of the Mexican nuns, exiled from their native country some years ago, can be worked into the picture. Naturally, I would like to see all this well on its way before I take my departure, so I have written Sister Caroline, asking if she wishes me to stay.

9

Perhaps one of Sister Catherine's greatest achievements in the apostolate of Children's Institutions was the erection of a new one on the "cottage plan" as a substitute for our old red brick Boyle Heights Orphanage in Los Angeles. It had been falling apart for years.

With no money in her pockets, Sister Catherine was sent to Los Angeles to "see what she could do." She writes of this assignment to her faithful friend, Sister Mary:

When I left Marillac very early in June no one dreamed that my stay out here would be such a prolonged one. Archbishop McIntyre demanded that someone come out to see what could be done about rebuilding the Orphanage and I happened to be the "someone" who could best be spared at the moment.

The project developed into three stages with many subdivisions: 1) Raise $750,000.00, 2) Find a new site, 3) Draw plans and get them approved by the various state and social agencies.

The second of these had us stopped so far as progress was concerned for four months. To find a site with sufficient acreage, close to the city, with accessibility to schools, and one where the zoning laws would permit the erection of a children's institution, presented undreamed of problems. Only last week did we come across one wholly desirable, and now we have started the legal machinery that will give us possession.

Would you believe, dear Sister Mary, that though we have the money in hand to pay for the place, and the owner is anxious to sell, it will take six weeks before the sale can be made? I wrote to Sister Caroline and suggested that she have a little shack put up on Marillac grounds where I could start a real estate business. There is not a thing I do not know now, not only as to the suitability of sites for different purposes, but I can also warn my clients against all legal pitfalls, such as, "restricted residence clause," "zoning variances," "oil and mineral rights retention," etc., etc. I hope to start back to Normandy about the middle of December, but I am not at all sure I can do so.

Sister Catherine did not succeed in getting away in December—it was June before she could leave. Writing to her brother-in-law some ten years later, she spoke man-to-man on the things Mr. Newton Stoer loved to discuss. It is one of the crosses that so often Sister had to carry with never a word about them, and always a cheerful "Blessed be God's Holy Will" in answer to those who would express their sympathy, that brought Sister Catherine close to this favorite brother-in-law.

He was the husband of Sister Catherine's sister, Constance, her only living sister. One evening, night rather, Constance had awakened with a dreadful headache, which she mentioned to her husband. He was frightened at the slurred way she spoke, and he suspected—what became tragically evident—that Constance had experienced a cerebral accident. He summoned an ambulance and took Constance to a Catholic Hospital in Shreveport, where she remained in a coma for eight years. Newton Stoer was heart-broken and visited the hospital twice a day, and kept three nurses round the clock to care for his wife. He bought for her the most fabulous negligees with slippers to match, not realizing that Constance, who had loved pretty and expensive clothes, would never have need for them again. His loving attention to Constance endured the entire eight years until her death.

Naturally, Sister Catherine appreciated this evidence of love and the longer Constance lived the greater devotion she felt for this brother-in-law.

We quote in full a letter that Sister Catherine wrote after Constance died and Mr. Newton Stoer was planning a trip to Los Angeles:

Dear Newt,

I must hasten to get my Christmas greetings to you since your letter of December 10 tells me that you will spend the Christmas holidays in Los Angeles with your sister, Mrs. J. G. Hester, and her family. I cannot tell you, Newt, how pleased I am that you have decided to do that. It will really make my Christmas happier, knowing that you are with your sister. I had the pleasure of meeting Mrs. Hester when I was in Los Angeles some ten years or so ago. She came to see me at the old Los Angeles Orphanage. I was very pleased to meet a member of your family, and, if I recall correctly, her own family is quite an interesting one. So, Newt dear, give your sister my love and my fond remembrance.

I spent a year in Los Angeles in the interest of raising funds for a new orphanage, there being an absolute necessity for replacing the old building on Boyle Heights which had long stood as a landmark in Los Angeles.

I discovered that I really had a talent as a fundraiser. Our initial estimate of the expense of a new orphanage was $750,000 and that seemed quite a large sum at the time. But, as we progressed, our own ideas as to what a modern children's home should be altered greatly, and, when the institution now known as Maryvale was finally completed, it was at a cost of $2,250,000. I smiled when I found out that all we owed on it was $750,000 or exactly what we first estimated the buildings would cost. That meant that we raised a million and a half.

In addition, we had made so many friends that we didn't feel at all anxious about the debt on the institution, and, as a matter of fact, it has long since been paid off.

Really, Newt, I wish you would just drive by Mary-vale, 7600 E. Graves Avenue, South San Gabriel. As Mrs. Hester will tell you, San Gabriel is a suburb of Los Angeles just about a 30-minute drive from the heart of the city. You will find it a modern, really beautiful "house of the Lord built for His least little ones." And please thank God for letting me be His real estate manager and planner!

Let me give you another tip, Newt, that may be handy, though I hope you won't need it during your stay in Los Angeles. We have St. Vincent's Hospital there, and, if you should need medical care, just mention my name and no matter how crowded they may be, they will find room for you and give you super attention. But, as I say, I hope you won't need it and that your visit with your sister will be wholly unclouded.

I presume you will take the trip by air which means, if you go jet flight, it will take just about three and a quarter hours. That is how long it took Sister Bertrande and me to come from San Francisco to St. Louis.

All goes well with Sister Bertrande and me and she frequently mentions you with great appreciation.

Devotedly yours,

SISTER CATHERINE

10

Although Sister Catherine always insisted that she had never had any real life-sized crosses to bear, it would seem that it depends on how one defines "crosses" and how one's viewpoint shapes one's attitudes. It is true that Sister Catherine had a wonderfully happy religious life, and she loved and treasured her vocation as a Daughter of Charity beyond all human blessings. She loved life almost voraciously and lived it to the full. I think the secret of her most unusual life was her steady growth into an almost superhuman conformity to the Will of God. It was by no easy process that she developed this actual, palpable love of God's Will, and recognized it in even the smallest vicissitudes, and even more especially in joyful events.

She was a humble person in her reactions to success, to high praise, to public acclaim. It never "went to her head." It just seemed that to her every moment was a special grace. If anyone said to her, and they often did, "Oh, Sister, God has greatly gifted you," she would answer: "Yes, Sister, I believe He has, so I must get back to work now, for that is what He gave me those gifts for—to work, not to stand and admire them."

Her secret for making life wonderful was that she accepted life on God's terms. What His terms were and how she accepted them on a certain Sunday afternoon in November, may be seen in this letter she wrote to Sister Mary Meehan late in November of 1951.

It will be no surprise to you when I say that, thanks to God's preventing grace, Sue's death occasioned me neither shock nor grief. Death is so much God's business that one simply bows unquestionably to the time, the manner and the place. I had talked to Sue over the phone just the previous evening; she lives in a little town just a hundred miles from Dallas. She was delighted to hear that I was so close and said that she and her husband would drive up either the next day or the day following.

I was expecting any minute that she would be announced that afternoon, when Sister Alberta Savage, the very devoted Sister Servant of St. Paul's, came into our room a little after three o'clock, saying, "I have terrible news."

Thinking she had just discovered that the fire damage was greater than at first estimated, I smilingly said: "What terrible news now, Sister?" There was no time for Sister to phrase her message in a preparatory way, so she replied at once, "Your dear sister Sue was killed and her husband critically injured in an auto accident on the way here. She has been taken to a funeral parlor and he is dying at Parkland Hospital."

I cannot express, dear Sister Mary, the peace, almost the exultation that filled my heart. "Sue dead . . . another loved one safe for all eternity."

I think my calmness puzzled and perhaps almost embarrassed Sister Alberta. I said aloud, "So Sue is dead. God rest her soul! Let us go first to the funeral parlor and then to Parkland Hospital." A priest had been sent for and he arrived at the funeral parlor just as we did. Although there were no signs of life and she had been pronounced dead, as it was less than an hour since the accident, Father anointed her.

For one fleeting moment I realized what I would have been without God's grace. From the merciful sheet that had been thrown over her body, wisps of bloodstained hair protruded; bits of shredded clothing hung down. The floor on which we knelt was wet from a hasty mopping—why that was necessary I knew all too well.

Just for a second I felt exactly as one would who, standing at a great height, suddenly felt all support withdrawn. But the emotion passed almost before it registered, and my silent ejaculations of "My Jesus mercy," "Lord have mercy on her soul" were infinitely peaceful. I kept whispering to my too rapid heart: "Be still, my heart, and listen to thy God."

From there we went to Parkland Hospital where her husband was being treated in the emergency room. We called a priest (a Vincentian, because the hospital is in their parish) to anoint Walter while the surgeons worked over him. He could not be moved from the table for five hours, so there was no question of transferring him to St. Paul's at that time. I notified his children—two daughters and two sons—all of whom live within one hundred and fifty miles of Dallas. They drove over with their wives and husbands, and also my sister Constance.

Sunday morning (the accident was Saturday afternoon) a family conference was held at St. Paul's to decide on the details of Sue's funeral. All were unanimous in deciding that she would wish to be buried by our parents in the family plot in Shreveport, Louisiana. Her husband could not be consulted as at that time we did not think that he knew Sue was dead—though we found out later that he did.

He remained fully conscious despite his injuries, giving my name and address to the ambulance driver who first reached the scene of the accident. The only reason he refrained from inquiring for several days about the accident was that he feared it might have been his fault. When he found out that it was caused by a drunken driver who turned his car into the wrong lane, dashing head-on into the Marshall's car, and that no amount of skill on his part could have saved Sue, an unbearable weight was lifted from his heart and he again found the will to try to live.

I am happy to say that, after hovering between life and death for several weeks, he is now on the road to recovery, though he will be in the hospital for another month or two. But he has been moved to St. Paul's and that means so much to all of us.

What Sister Catherine was never to know (though perhaps she does now) is the result of her soldierly self-discipline. It would be only natural to most of us to lift the sheet for one brief look at Sue's loved face. She, of all the sisters, resembled Sister Catherine the most. But she did not touch the sheet. She knelt with tear-filled eyes, upright, and in perfect control. Had she raised just a corner of the sheet, she would have found no face at all.

Alert, intelligent Sister Alberta told the mortician that Sister Catherine and Sue were perfect look-alikes; so quietly and unobtrusively, the mortician's artist sketched Sister Catherine as she knelt as still as stone.

Later Sister Catherine and all the relatives said, as they gazed at Sue in her coffin: "Oh, isn't she natural?" and they murmured their gratitude that her face had been unhurt. But one of the family said: "Sister Catherine, I told Sue just last week that every day she resembled you more and more. It pleased her very much."

Months later, in speaking of Sue, Sister Catherine said, "It was a perfect miracle that Sue could look so peaceful. And do you know she was the image of me!"

EIGHT

On January 26, 1952, Sister Caroline Collins, so beloved by the entire province, died of an infirmity that she had borne with unbelievable stamina for more than half of her Community life. Her biography has been written and shows once again the tremendous "soldiers" formed to the religious life by Sister Augustine Parks and her predecessors.

On March 15, 1952 (anniversary of her First Vows), Sister Catherine Sullivan was installed as the third Visitatrix of the St. Louis Province. Her varied and prolonged experience in each of our different works made her an honest-to-goodness wonder-woman, for no Sister in any of our far-flung works ever found Sister Catherine "stumped"—whether it was a problem in public-private school relations; whether it was hospitals becoming entangled with medicare, medicaid, data processing, child care, or geriatrics. She knew them all, for she had been there. It is, I think, safe to say that no one had ever come to the duty of Visitatrix better prepared, and with better credentials. She was acknowledged over the province as the "most spiritual Sister" in it. Her experience at Carville in dealing with the government at Washington (called to join in many conferences with the Surgeon General, asked advice of by prominent leaders, making lasting friends of almost every professional contact) proved not only invaluable to all Communities as well as our own, but is a tribute to her boundless zeal in promoting the work of the Church in every way that came to hand.

Moreover, Sister Catherine had an accomplished secretary, Sister Margaret Mary O'Connor, whom she trained to be much more than secretary, for something new was to be learned every day—and Sister Margaret Mary learned to anticipate Sister Catherine's wishes, and carried them out with the same competent zeal that prompted each action of Sister Catherine's. There was a perfect and loving rapport between them, so that it can honestly be said that Sister Catherine could not have accomplished all she did were it not for Sister Margaret Mary's loyal and effective support.

1

This preface is to turn over to the reader the task of answering the question: "What do you think is the greatest contribution Sister Catherine made during her long years of service (fifty-eight of which were strenuously active) to society—especially in her ten years as Visitatrix?" It is a ticklish question. For the preceding chapter has shown, only partially, how extremely active she was in all the various apostolates, some that she herself initiated, and those she renewed in spirit and effectiveness.

One Sister, at the close of Sister's term as Visitatrix, said: "Well, I guess this doesn't sound like much depth of thought, but I am going to say it anyhow. I think the greatest gift Sister Catherine gave to our province was in changing the hour of rising from four o'clock to five A.M. Now, go ahead and say I am selfish; but, before you do, listen to what that one act did for me. First, I got eight hours of sleep, so I was alert for my morning meditation which began at 5:30. And that is true throughout the province. For practically all of us, meditation was a constant struggle against sleep. You hardly ever see a head nodding in drowsiness now. Secondly, I do much better in the classroom. I don't arrive there sluggish with lack of sleep. I could go on and on."

Sister Catherine was steadfastly interested in promoting a fervent prayer life in the Community; and it was stepped up at the change in the hour of rising. It was noticeable throughout the province how much stronger and steadier the Sisters tried to help one another, encouraged by Sister Catherine, to take advantage of all the graces and help to be derived from prayer, and most especially mental prayer. But few people knew of the active opposition Sister met so courageously in making this gigantic departure from the three hundred year traditional hour of four o'clock rising. But she tossed off any sympathy offered with: "Everything has its price."

2

Then there will be those who will say her greatest contribution to the Church and religious life was when, as vice-chairman, to a much older but very active Mother General Chairman, she helped form the very first National Congress of Major Superiors of Womens' Institutes. It acquainted her with practically every religious congregation in the United States and Canada. And, when she went as delegate to the first Congress of Religious Superiors, she made so favorable an impression that she was the one named to those Cardinals and Bishops and Mothers General who were asking for details of Sister Formation as it progressed with "Americans." She used to laugh about it in retrospect, saying: "I felt like setting up a little cashier-cage office on a street corner with a sign over it: HOW THE AMERICANS DO IT—for Rome especially was visibly interested in our Catholic School System, which gave me a wonderful opportunity to talk on my favorite subject— Sisters."

But those who know Sister Catherine best insist that the greatest gift she was given, and exercised so well as the years went on, was a deep and abiding faith in the Church that Christ left us as His greatest legacy. Over and over she would remind the Sisters: "Remember, dear Sisters, Saint Vincent constantly urged us to be true Daughters of the Church. When the Pope speaks, he speaks as our Lord inspires him to speak, and, if we keep close to the Church, we shall be close to Christ Who promised to be with it always. If we do this in all crises that threaten our faith, what have we to fear?"

Perhaps Sister Catherine's single greatest achievement was the founding of the first *Liberal Arts College for Sisters Only*—Marillac College. Those who don't or won't get the point of a college for Sisters only, do not perceive the wisdom in Sister Catherine's philosophy: "Sisters are different. It is ridiculous to educate them in the same way and by the same secular standards as lay people in lay colleges and then expect them to live as Christ called them to live—as He lived—which is the whole point of their holy vocation."

Still another school of thought will say that Sister Catherine's greatest contribution to the religious life in particular, and perhaps to lay people as well, is the constant encouragement she brought to Sisters of all Communities all over the country when both Catholic and secular journalists (and the adjective "arrogant" should be inserted before the antecedent noun) began giving the Sisters a bad time with articles and books asking: "Should Religious Life Survive?" and "Has the Religious Life Served Its Purpose—Is It Relevant Today?", all of which was calculated to deter girls from entering the convent, and tempting those who were in the convent to leave.

Sister Catherine thought this "bad time" was good for all of us. She predicted that it would separate the chaff from the wheat. But she deplored the harm it would so mendaciously bring about in confusing the reading public—Catholics as well as non-Catholics.

3

She gave countless lectures to all-Sister audiences, in an endeavor to help them to search their own souls, but especially to search between the lines of these vicious articles designed to delight the "itching ears" of the discontented, and trouble souls that had hitherto rejoiced in their holy vocation. Of those articles that insisted rudely and crudely that Sisters were no longer relevant to the Church, she would ask her audiences of Sisters: "Who says we're not relevant? Name the expert who truly knows whereof he speaks. Our Holy Father Pius XII said, what Paul VI repeated later:

> The apostolate of the Church today is scarcely conceivable without the cooperation of religious women

in works of charity, in hospitals, in schools, in assistance to the priestly ministry, in the missions.

"Yes," Sister Catherine insisted, "without Sisters to staff them, the vast majority of our schools, hospitals, children's institutions, settlements, day nurseries, would close their doors. Almost every mail brings to me a plea for Sisters for this or that work. We had thirty-five such requests this summer—we accepted one. And that, Sisters, points up what a lost or a rejected vocation means. If a girl has a call to be a Daughter of Charity and through cowardice, lack of generosity, or love of the world rejects it, it means something very much more than that one soul has missed the path of perfection to which she was called.

"It means that children who should have been instructed in the Faith and kept close to Our Lord and His Blessed Mother must attend secular schools from which even the name of God is banished; it means that the sick and dying do not have the aid of the sacraments and the comfort of their religion; it means that children deprived of a natural family life are deprived also of the love, affection and understanding, which God destined them to find in the hearts of Sisters; it means that the poor and the friendless and the needy and the discouraged have no one to show them how to sanctify their suffering but must depend upon the cold, unfeeling charity of the State, which only too often embitters while it gives material help.

"Ah yes, dear Sisters, a person who is unfaithful to a religious vocation is like a person appointed to keep burning a lamp in a lighthouse, located by dangerous waters. If the keeper decides that he is tired or cold or bored or lonesome and deserts his post—what happens? The light goes out and the ships that counted on its guiding light are dashed on the rocks and perish. Sisters, we can live our own life, if we want; but we must also die our own death—and face our own judgment.

"You know, Sisters," she continued, "some of us make far too much of the trials of Community life and we talk too much and too glibly about the 'sacrifices of a religious life.' Someone has said that the exodus of mothers from their homes to offices and factories is due largely to their having heard *their* mothers complain about the drudgery of housework and 'A woman's work is never done,' and they resolved not to be stuck with that.

"Perhaps the fewness of religious vocations can be attributed, in a measure, to the impression some of us give that the religious life is a slow and drab form of martyrdom. 'You have to get up awful early.' Yes? Millions of farmers and dairy men get up hours ahead of us and go out into a cold barn to milk twenty cows because their living depends upon it. You may be tempted to be sorry for yourself because you have fifty-two children in a parish school. Do you ever stop to think, Sisters, that there are lay teachers who teach as hard as you do all day, and then go home and cook, wash, and look after a family—and *then* prepare their lessons for the next day? Or you're in a hospital and you've 'been on night duty *two* months.' Terrible, isn't it?

"Look out the window and see the poor policeman tramping the icy streets, or the pavements hot even at night, in the teeming rain, and under the necessity of being always ready to risk his life at a moment's notice. Think of the watchmen who have spent years at the monotonous task of just watching—then go home to sleep and rest without a chance to get more than half acquainted with their wives and children. Or, you are a student now. You have this and that class and this and that assignment. Many and many a girl in the world has to hold down a job while getting her education, and perhaps after a night class, getting home at 10:00 P.M. she has to cook and wash and get ready for her job the next day.

"Our Blessed Lord promised us a hundredfold even in this world. He gives it. Let us at least be grateful. Let cheerfulness be our watchword. A good motto might be, as I once heard a Sister with a pronounced Southern accent, say: 'No mo' moanin' Lawd, no mo' moanin'. And we might very profitably meditate on the words of a Baptist Minister with an even stronger Southern accent:

> You cain't do as you pleases
> If you wants to walk with Jesus."

Sister Catherine took an avid interest in Renewal after Vatican II had spoken through the documents and decrees of the Conciliar Fathers. These documents and decrees she could quote almost by heart, especially those that pertain to the religious life. Across the country she would speak to troubled Communities, as well as to our own. Come to think of it, this sensitive interest to all that concerned the Church and religious life within its framework, could very well compete as one of the greatest contributions Sister Catherine made to the Church.

"Dear Sisters," she would say, "do not get frightened or confused about this 'changing world' of which we hear and read from morning until night. The world has always been changing. It began changing in the Garden of Eden, think that over. What a change for our first parents! It will go on changing until the final battle on the field of Armageddon, which Scripture tells us will signal the end of the world. In things that pertain to time, we *must* change with the world. In those things that pertain to eternity, we dare not change."

4

Sister Catherine was all for controlled change that would revivify religious life; but she did not think the baby had to be thrown out with the bath water in order to effect the changes we all know need to be made. Sister had a deep sympathy for those who acted like children that had been held down too tightly under maternal control, and then, when the heavy hand was lifted, went wild—and, if we are absolutely honest, we will admit that. But perhaps this was not a greater disturbance to peace, harmony, and brotherly love than that made by pious obstinacy on the part of those who did not wish to make the tiniest change from worn out, outmoded traditions that, if looked at with honest intelligence, no longer made any contribution, but rather served as obstacles to true Community life. Ominously, these obstructionists predicted: "Give them an inch and they'll take a mile." Some did, as a matter of fact, take several acres.

Who should be the arbiter? Certainly not the journalists we mentioned before; certainly not young priests who—sad to say—were heady with what they considered as their destiny to reform the Church. Sister Catherine gave an answer to this question when she spoke to the

44th convention of the National Catholic Hospital Association of the United States and Canada:

We do indeed face the challenge of change. But a challenge connotes a challenger, and the challenge is important only in proportion to the honor, dignity, integrity and power of the challenger. Who has thrown down the glove to us—who with the proper credentials of honor, dignity, integrity, and power, has thrown down the gauntlet to all religious of the world?

Is it the State? Licensing Bureau? Social Agencies? Educational accrediting groups, national and regional? The White House? No! The challenge, urgent, imperative, demanding, comes from the highest possible source. It comes from His Holiness, the Spiritual Leader and the Teaching Authority of the Church, the Vicar of Christ on earth, the highest Superior of every individual Religious. The challenge has been made by him who is our first superior, to whom our Vow of Obedience is made, and to whom we owe absolute allegiance. Whoever repudiates him, repudiates Christ whom he represents.

We cannot be too deeply imbued with this truth, Sisters, for accepting the Holy Father's challenge means change, adaptation, conformity—all in virtue of the obedience we owe to the Holy See. Sisters, it is trite, it is mouthing a cliché to say that the world is changing. The world began changing in the Garden of Eden—changing violently—and it will go on changing until it reaches the Field of Armageddon. But what *is* startling and peculiar to our era is that this is the first time in the history of the Church that its Supreme Head has urged Communities to change, to adapt their mode of life and manner of service to the needs of the world as it is today.

Dear Sisters, whose voice but that of the Pope could have penetrated the hallowed halls of our Mother

141

Houses, reaching into Community Council rooms to bring about modifications in Constitutions, Rules and Customs, while keeping the spirit intact? Whose hand but that of Christ's Vicar could have cut away the dead wood of tradition from each Community Tree, in order that it might bear fruit more abundantly? No one else could have done it. No one else would have had the right to do it. His very title has a significant application to those of us who have renounced the world, and yet must work out our salvation by serving that same world.

Our Holy Father has found the way; he built the bridge. How we need the security that derives from familiarity with his writings, addresses, directives and allocutions. They should be used for spiritual lectures, for refectory readings, for discussion amongst us in study groups. Let us remember that every Community came into existence to serve the Church, and it is axiomatic that "Where the Pope is, there is the Church."

Sisters, do we sufficiently appreciate our great privilege in being a Religious in this day and era? I have been a Religious for more than fifty years, and I am ready to say to our Blessed Lord, "Thou hast kept the good wine until now." Never before in the history of the Church has a Supreme Pontiff been so engrossed with Religious Communities. Never before has a Pope issued so many instructions concerning Religious and their way of life, or manifested such an affection for them.

Once I was privileged to hear him say, in reference to the one million Religious in the world: "Oh, that I had all those Religious in my hands; I need them!" Think of it, Sisters, the Holy Father says he *needs* us. Does it not remind you of St. Paul's saying, "The head cannot say to the hand, 'I have no need of you'." Or

1

The news was made public to the province during the annual retreat of all the Sister Servants of the province in January. On January 29, 1962 her successor, Sister Mary Rose McPhee, was installed. No one in the entire province was happier or more pleased with the appointment of Sister Mary Rose than Sister Catherine herself. She told me with her stunning blue eyes shining, "I prayed for this for two years."

She left almost immediately—without a tear in her eye—for Los Angeles where she was to rest for several months before taking up an assignment as Province Director of Vocations, in Chicago. The Sister Servant of St. Vincent Hospital, Los Angeles, Sister Fidelis Klein, was a long-time friend of Sister Catherine; she had been on mission at Charity Hospital, New Orleans, while Sister Catherine had been at Carville. Insofar as she could manage it, she gave Sister Catherine the earth with a golden fence around it—and this was a personal joy to Sister Fidelis herself even more than to Sister Catherine, because Sister Fidelis knew how to love unobtrusively, and to give of material comforts in the same way. She wept the day that Sister Mary Rose, Visitatrix, came to take Sister Catherine to Chicago with her. Sister had improved a great deal; but doing nothing, she often said, made her feel that she was on another planet.

It was not for long that she did nothing. She set to work building up, so that the day after she arrived in Chicago, her typewriter was clacking away. With thoughtful kindness—and it is possible to be very kind without being the least bit thoughtful—Sister Mary Rose provided a Sister-Secretary for her, and in no time at all a flourishing business was going on at the Office of the Province Director of Vocations.

2

In the meantime, architects, carpenters, builders were at work on the fourth (top) floor at Marillac Provincial House, transforming it into a new series of offices, conference rooms, waiting rooms, etc. for the Vocation Office. 'Twas the night after Christmas when Father Dolan, Spiritual Director of the Province, led a procession for the ceremony of blessing what Sister Catherine quickly christened The Daughters of Charity Information Office—and what a beautiful, functional series of tastily furnished rooms they were.

Just above us were the spires of Marillac (the architecture circa 1910). Sister Catherine christened for short the entire top floor given to us as "The Towers"; and we used to kid each other about being the "Two Princes"—waiting to have our heads cut off. But there were more than just the two of us. Sister Catherine had, as her confidential secretary, Sister Lois Douglass, and a lay secretary. I had Sister Marie Sheehy as assistant and Mrs. Georgia Casey as secretary. It would be difficult to say which was the fastest at taking dictation and transcribing—all were perfect; and put out an extraordinary amount of work each day. Since Sister Catherine's office faced mine we practically faced each other at work and held frequent conferences about our joint enterprises. Only God knows and understands what it means now to look at a closed door down a short cor-

efforts expended purposefully, that our entire life is a fulfilling of the orders of our Commander-in-Chief.

It is a temptation to include several other editorials— but the three chosen give adequate testimony to Sister Catherine's fertile imagination and many-faceted mind.

4

What would make a three-volume tome would be her letters, written to many and various people. They run the whole gamut of humanity: from Trappists to Bishops in the clerical world; and in the lay world, from the former children of St. Rose's to the women (some now near her own age) who had been nurses with her at Dallas, Waco, and St. Thomas Hospital in Nashville, Tennessee; and in the world of religious women, from Mothers General to novices whose Directresses had suggested they write to her as a woman of wisdom who could and would help them with a personal problem. But to the Sisters of her own Community she gave first place. Any letter received today, if it were important, would have an answer within two days. Where a Sister was weighed down with anxiety and doubt, Sister Catherine telephoned the answer no matter how many miles intervened. Of course these recipients of letters from Sister Catherine did not individually average more than two or three letters a year at most. But certain it is, if her letters were to be printed they could not be contained in one volume.

For Sister Catherine, letter-writing was as truly an apostolate of delicate charity as was visiting the widow bereft of her husband in a tragic accident or visiting the sick in their homes or in hospitals. Sister Catherine attended wakes of deceased relatives of the Sisters as faithfully as she attended Mass on Sunday.

Her relationships with people were always on a very personal basis. In the days when "particular" friendships were the *bete noir* of most retreat masters, religious superiors and the subject of many spiritual writers, Sister Catherine never spoke of them. Once a Sister said to Sister Catherine: "What do you think of these so-called 'particular friendships' we hear so much about?" Airily she quipped: "Particular friendships? *Why all of my friends are particular.*"

One of Sister Catherine's most favorite people—as she would call it—was her personal physician, Dr. David B. Flavan. Sister never traded on personal friendship to get professional concessions. She always asked his permission for any extensive travel, because she was a cardiac hazard. When Sister was going to Rome for the conferring of the red hat on Cardinal Ritter, she consulted Dr. Flavan. He looked grave. "You know you're not getting any younger, Sister, though you hold your own very well. I'll have to lay down a condition for your going. You may go on one condition, and that is, provided you take your personal physician with you."

Dr. Flavan is almost abnormally busy; but work could wait while he (and his wife) went to Rome, with Cardinal-elect Ritter and his by-invitation-only retinue, to keep on eye on Sister Catherine's health.

When I asked Dr. Flavan if I might include a personal letter or two from Sister Catherine, he launched on a eulogy of her subtle wit, the jokes they shared, and—as everybody who knew her—rhapsodies of what a wonderful woman she was. When I came back to the original request, he hedged:

"Sister," he said, "do you know where those letters are now?"

I hazarded, "In your files?"

He said, "No, they are in my special box in the bank vault. I go down there and read them sometimes when I need a lift. Nobody has a key to that box but *ME*. Absolutely nobody."

I teased: "Are you leading up to saying 'no'?"

With real regret, but a kindly firmness, he said: "I'm afraid so. They're sacred to me, Sister."

Dr. Flavan had served Sister Catherine for more than thirty years; I know that she counted Dr. David B. Flavan and Mrs. Flavan among her close friends.

5

Another revered but informal friend is now dead, Monsignor John J. Butler. We venture that in Heaven he will look kindly on one's pilfering just one letter to Sister Catherine and her answer, which summarizes so many of the works they accomplished together.

From the Rt. Rev. Msgr. Butler:

Sister Catherine, D.C.
Marillac Seminary
Normandy, Missouri

Dear Sister Catherine:

Enclosed is the "address" which you wanted to read. As a matter of fact, you are the first to receive a copy. I know it doesn't come up to some of the gems of which you are capable yourself—but it is rather difficult to express in ten minutes the tremendous dedication of forty-eight years.

I find it just as difficult, even now, to express to you, my dear friend, the thoughts that flood heart and mind at such a time in my life. To say that it is a rare privilege to work with you personally and with the Daughters of Charity is a very mild statement indeed. We have certainly ploughed through many a rough spot together, but on the other hand, we have shared a lot of joy. How does one say "thank you" for generosity, for understanding, for friendship through many years except to say from the bottom of a very full heart, "God bless you now and always."

Sincerely and gratefully in Our Lord,

A week later to the day, Monsignor received this response from Sister Catherine:

Rt. Rev. Msgr. John J. Butler, President
The Catholic Charities of St. Louis
2331 Mullanphy Street
Saint Louis 6, Missouri

Dear Monsignor Butler:

Life has its moments. Rare. Unplanned. Unpredictable. Such a moment was mine, dear Monsignor Butler, when I read your letter that accompanied the promised copy of your talk at the Testimonial Dinner recently tendered in your honor.

Moments are utterly dissociated with years, so time stood still, or rather, the past, present and future blended into a three-dimensional picture in which I viewed our working together during the past twenty-one years. Vignettes stand out: Just you and I in your office discussing certain immediately needed repairs to Guardian Angel Settlement—a matter of only a few thousand dollars but it seemed awfully big to us then—and your termination of the interview by reaching into a drawer of your desk, and passing me the amount needed with an almost apologetic remark: "I happen to have it."

Then, the hurry-up necessity during World War II to establish a Day Nursery sent us both to exploring the possibilities of space at St. Philomena's. "This will serve as a dining room, and these rooms as dormitories, and this for a playroom. . . ." Within ten days, Stella Maris Day Nursery was ready for applicants. Do you remember getting a telephone call from a newspaper reporter, asking: "Who is this Mrs. Stella Morris that established the Day Nursery named after her?"

Most brilliant of all the vignettes is that of the Child Guidance Center of Our Lady of Grace, which came into existence solely because of your vision and of the acute need for it—and my desire to follow your leadership. Money was needed, we said, and personnel. We had neither—like Peter and John when accosted by a beggar for alms. Like the Apostles, also, we said: "But what we have, we give you." Our knowledge of the need, and the firm faith that if we make a beginning, in the name of Christ, "He who has begun the good work will perfect it unto the end." And so it was.

How fitting that the financial returns from the Testimonial Dinner should go to the Child Center of Our Lady of Grace, your work of predilection. Nothing could have been more appropriate.

Your speech is a masterpiece, dear Monsignor Butler. As I read it, I marveled at its structure, its flashes of wit here, its subtle irony there, but withal its able expression of your affectionate gratitude for all of the persons who have worked so zealously and ably under your direction. Dear Monsignor Butler, I was joyously proud when I found my name amongst those you specially mentioned as your friends. But for the rest of my life I shall be humbly grateful that my name will be mentioned by you to your First Friend, our Blessed Lord, the Source and Model of all charity.

Devotedly,

We quote from Sister Catherine's letter to Father Miller, successor to Monsignor Butler as President of Catholic Charities of St. Louis:

Reverend John W. Miller
Saint Louise de Marillac Rectory
Jennings, Missouri

Dear Father Miller,

I am rather glad that I was absent from the city when the announcement of your appointment as Director of Catholic Charities was made, because I prefer that my congratulations be not mingled with nor lost in the deluge of such notes and messages that you must have received.

Director of Catholic Charities of the Archdiocese of St. Louis is a tremendously important job, viewed from any angle. But it becomes awesomely portentous when one thinks of it in relation to the thousands of poor and needy of all kind which become now your special charges. Yes, yours, Father, because no matter how well organized and administered an agency is, the final responsibility rests in the hands—and heart—of the one who holds the chief position. Yours the infant and the derelict, yours the dependent child and the still more dependent aged, yours the juvenile delinquent and the struggling widow, yours the homeless and the hungry. Your assignment brings to full fruition your ordination as Deacon, and may Stephen, Philip, Prochorus, Nicanor, Timon, Parmenas and Nicholas assist you.

I am sending to Paris some Mass offerings for your intentions, dear Father Miller, and I am specifying that one Mass be offered in the Sacred Heart Basilica at Montmarte, that the "Sacred Heart of Jesus, of Whose fulness we have all received," may impart a special degree of that fulness to you. Another Mass is to be offered at the Shrine of St. Vincent de Paul in the Vincentian Motherhouse, that the Patron of all Charitable Works may be ever mindful of you. Another Mass is to be offered at the Shrine of St. Louise de Marillac, in the Miraculous Medal Chapel. Certainly she has had a special interest in you, dear Father Miller, ever since *you were appointed* assistant Pastor in the parish dedicated to her. But in addition I have a very special intention in that Mass at St. Louise's altar: It is that she will bless you with an understanding, sympathy and tact in dealing with *all religious women*. Not a small boon, that! The fourth Mass is to be offered at the Shrine of Saint Catherine Laboure, that your happy relations with the Daughters will ever continue.

Sincerely,

Sister Catherine's subtle concern for *all religious women* will not be lost on the reader. It was characteristic of her to love all the Sisters of the world, and willingly would she have made any sacrifice for them.

TEN

Sister Catherine loved life; she did not want to die. She was not at all afraid of death; she often said she would gladly welcome it when the time came, but she was in no hurry for it to arrive. "Life is so interesting," she would say, "especially now when no one knows what's going to happen next." She had an unconquerable interest in everything. Baseball, for one example. She rarely, and only on a holiday, would follow the game on television or radio, but in picking up the newspaper for a run-down of the news each morning she turned to the Sports section first to see what the Cardinals were doing.

And our space efforts; the astronauts were like brothers to her, and she often remarked that she prayed for their brave wives. She must have had all Heaven watching the moon when we planted the flag there. She read the editorials and the columnists—agreed or disagreed aloud, and then with a salute to another new day, she would begin her morning's round of dictation at eight o'clock until noon. Her secretaries loved her and speaking of her unfailing sense of humor they would say: "It's like reading a new and absorbing book every day with each new letter dictated seeming like a new and exciting next chapter."

But her abiding interest was the Church and the religious life. She was delighted that all religious were experimenting in ways and means of how to get rid of

164

the cobwebs that had accumulated around rules, customs and once worthy but now outmoded traditions. But it disquieted her to see the secular forms some of the experiments were taking. She was a keen student of human nature, a loving and understanding one, but her last days were shadowed by what was happening to some Communities due to what she attributed to a faulty reading and misinterpretation of the post-conciliar decrees.

But one never heard a word of destructive criticism from her about priests or Sisters; simply she prayed for them. Nothing daunted her faith; it was just the suffering of the Holy Father, and the turmoil in the Church that disturbed her. But always the cheery words: "The Church and religious will go on forever—those who leave, lose; those who stay are the winners. Oh Sisters," she would add, "let us pray very hard for the losers." Then with a roguish smile, and a twinkle in her eyes, she would implore: "But don't ever say of them that 'they meant well' .... It is the one calumny or detraction I could never endure. Just imagine having 'She meant well' inscribed on your tombstone!"

1

Sister's health was failing, as one might expect at her age; but from October through December, she was in and out of DePaul Hospital, with a back ailment that Dr. Flavan ascribed to stress. "You want to work at eight-two," he said, "as you did at fifty, and no—it cannot be done."

Sister Catherine came home from the hospital on New Year's Eve. She was very much her old self, saying that

Dr. Flavan had condemned her to an armchair. Obedient, as always, honoring the physician because we all have need of him, she took to reading again like a rocket to the moon. It was a restful period for Sister Catherine; but love is psychic. I said to her one day, early in January: "My premonitions never come true, no matter how strong they are—but I have a foreboding in my heart that we won't be together much longer."

Always the spiritual optimist, she said: "But think of the long years we've had together! And what wonderful years they were! Let us thank God for them—I do daily. And just think, we'll have all eternity together." And, after a pause, she added: "And let's make the most of the time we have left."

This was the nearest she came to any mention of death.

On January 24 her breathing became labored, and she had to wear an oxygen mask almost three hours out of four. When her difficulty in breathing abated, even for only half an hour, she would—of all things—read.

On January 25, however, the breathing difficulty became very grave. Sister lost consciousness and about four o'clock was rushed to DePaul Hospital in a dying condition. She was immediately placed in the cardiac intensive care unit. Sister nurses worked with her around the clock, and managed almost miraculously to make her comfortable, so that she seemed at peace and free from pain. The morning of the day she died, I slipped into her room, and whispered to her: "Sister, am I getting through to you?" She spoke my name, and added a few words that will remain locked in my heart forever. Now that she is gone and "her place knows her no more" I cling to the memory of those words to help me with whatever time is left ahead.

As I left the room, her day nurse, Sister Esther Levan, followed me outside. "Sister," she said, "yesterday afternoon Sister roused from a sleep, opened her big blue eyes to their widest, and as though she were greeting someone she loved, she said almost in her own, usually strong voice: 'Mamie! Oh Mamie!' Then she smiled and lay back on her pillow. Who is Mamie?" Sister Esther asked. I answered briefly: "Her favorite sister who died years ago."

2

That night, with no struggle, just with a sigh, Sister Catherine Sullivan died, just one month from completing sixty happy years as a Daughter of Charity. At her own request she was buried among the Sisters, "At the next vacant place." She had added, "Don't set me apart with the dignitaries," referring, no doubt, to the special graves, with larger tombstones, of the two former Visitatrices, a tribute from the Sisters, which they had not had the foresight to forestall.

Thanks to the "new liturgy" which Sister Catherine loved, our Reverend Spiritual Director, Father George Dolan, C.M., insisted on no black Mass. "For Sister Catherine" he said, "only the Easter Mass of the Resurrection is fitting. And only Joy, because she herself was the spirit of joy, is a fitting theme for our last farewell."

At her funeral Mass, Father Dolan gave the homily. In his opening remarks he called attention to the brochure (Liturgy Mass of Burial for Sister Catherine Sullivan, D.C.) in which was given the explanation for the choice of the Mass of the Resurrection:

> Today's liturgy, like the reality of Christian death, is a mixture of the sorrow and sense of loss and the constant unconquered hope of resurrection. The white vestments, the paschal candle, the whole positive tone of the liturgy—all of these speak to us of the ultimate victory of Christ. For we have come together to honor a life spent in the service of Christ and His Mystical Body. We testify by our belief and confidence that this life is not ended, but merely changed. This is the fruition of Christian life; the white robe given at Baptism becomes the white cloth of resurrection covering the coffin. A new, unending life is begun, and we are called to profess our faith in our sharing a similar destiny with God.

In speaking of Sister Catherine's many accomplishments Father Dolan said:

> The list of services which Sister Catherine rendered to the Church was rather formidable and, if we reflect upon the contribution she made to the Church, to the Community, and to individuals both within the Community and outside—be they members of other Communities or be they members of the laity in various contacts with her—her works were astounding.

He then likened her to a "candle-bearer" thus:

> In reflecting on Sister Catherine one thought in particular keeps returning and that is the thought of Sister Catherine as a candle-bearer—one who sheds light and cheer and warmth and love; one who was always so optimistic; one who tried so successfully to do the Will of God, and, because of her faith and hope and love of God was able always to see the bright side, the cheery side of life and circumstances. With Sister

Catherine it was never partly cloudy; it was partly sunshine. With Sister Catherine a half-filled glass of water was never half-empty; it was half full.

One day in the wintertime years ago, standing at the front door, while talking to several of the Sisters, one of them remarked how bare were the trees. But Sister, in her cheerfulness, optimism, and warmth, said: "Yes, it is good that the trees are bare. This way we can see the trees because they are not hidden with their foliage."

Sister Catherine certainly was proof that it is better to light one candle and help extinguish the darkness than to light no candle and curse the darkness. For no matter what the circumstances were, no matter how suddenly a particular situation developed, no matter how seemingly impossible the situation was—Sister Catherine always called on her faith, her hope, and her love of God, and, in her attempts to live in conformity with the Will of God, was always able to see the light.

This is why I think of her as a "candle-bearer."

Tributes poured in. From among the many Bishops, Monsignori, Priests, Mothers General, private Sister friends, and friends among the laity we have chosen two:

3

One of Sister Catherine's close friends, in far off India, Sister Beatrice Brown, D.C., now President of St. Justin College—which, by the way, is open only to students who already possess the Bachelor or Master's degree, but need courses in newer techniques in teaching—writes:

No one in all the world, not even you, Sister, knows how much I owe Sister Catherine for being what she is and what she has meant to me all these years. One can only repay her with what she so much deserves— a deep and enduring love, which I give her with all my heart.

I have two little banners in my steel cupboard in my bedroom. Each night, before I retire, I gaze on them lovingly, because they so forcefully remind me of our precious Sister Catherine.

The first banner announces: "We are molded by those who love us." What an artist, what a sculptor she was! The second banner reads: "The Church relies on you."

What a force for good was Sister Catherine! Above all, in molding Sisters to love and obedience to the Church, which guarantees that in our humble, human way we can prove our supernatural love of God!

SISTER CATHERINE SULLIVAN, D.C.

By Sister Mary Emil Penet, I.H.M.
(Monroe, Michigan)

Sister Catherine Sullivan, D.C., who died on February 1, was the second National Chairman of the Sister Formation Conference. She was a member of the national leadership group for about a decade. During these years there was a firm hand at the helm in national planning, and the National Chairman brought to each meeting a blend of sparkle and wisdom that are not often joined. Her interest in Sister Formation as an organization began with the very first regional conference, which the Midwest held in Chicago in 1954. With Sister Catherine, interest meant support, and her name was always high on the list of major superiors who gave the Conference status and security when the ideas for which it stood were still struggling for acceptance. For these contributions alone any of us who cherish the movement should be saddened by the passing of one of its most clear-sighted leaders and staunchest friends.

Yet Sister Catherine's formal participation in the organization was perhaps not her greatest contribution to the Sister Formation movement. That contribution was her founding, together with Sister Bertrande Meyers, of Marillac College in St. Louis, a unique center for the education of Sisters of all Communities, which today boasts of a faculty representing fifteen different religious orders, and a student body of just under 500, representing thirty-seven congregations. The inter-community faculty and inter-community student body, and the limitation to religious students could have been seen as temporary measures and could have been handled as expediencies. With Sister Catherine, however, these features of Marillac, from its beginning to the present time, have been developed as cherished strengths—never to be abandoned no matter what difficulty or expense the cooperative approach might necessitate.

The visitor to Marillac College—which won regional accreditation almost immediately, followed by NLN (National Leage of Nurses) and in due time NCATE (National Council for the Accreditation of Teacher Education)—will be struck by the largeness of vision and attention to detail which went into its planning. What this really means is that Sister Catherine, Visitatrix during most of the building period, approached Sister Formation as a true community work of the Daughters of Charity, one deserving of every improvement and facility, an apostolate to the poor in the truest sense, because it was destined to form the servants of the poor. As servants of the poor bearing the

171

charisms of many different founders and foundresses will continue to go out from Marillac College, they should know how to combine largeness of view with intensity of purpose, and if they continue to achieve that combination, they will owe more than they themselves realize to the woman who dreamed and planned and supported this institution.

But even beyond what all of us owe Marillac, those of us of other communities who were privileged to know and work with Sister Catherine, are indebted to her for what she was. What she was is hard to explain, for Sister Catherine broke all the molds. With charm and tact and exquisite obedience she broke them. And although she suffered fools gladly, none of us were with her very long without being separated skillfully from at least a little of our foolishness.

When intellectual interests were somewhat suspect among sisters, Sister Catherine was a reader, and by her own efforts became a scholar. Among other things, she was a Scripture scholar—decades before that became fashionable. Living through an era of specialization in which there really should not have been crossovers in professions, she won national eminence for pioneering work with Hansen's disease in the leprosarium at Carville, where she spent twenty years; she attained top leadership positions in the National Conference of Catholic Charities because of her subsequent work with unwed mothers; she was an officer in both the Conference of Major Religious Superiors and the National Sister Formation Conference, and she proved an able and astute administrator of a far-flung province of hospitals, schools, and social agencies spread over half a continent and which included Japan, Formosa and Puerto Rico. At an age when the books call for retirement she founded a college and served as its first President. When renewal came along and suggested liberty of spirit, Sister Catherine agreed impishly because she had always had it. When Sister Bertrande wrote a best seller denouncing formalism, Sister Catherine applauded, although she herself had never suffered from that disease. When "new-think," a few years later proceeded to threaten the destruction of Catholic education, and introduced some secularization of religious life, Sister Catherine was not threatened by thought-fashions which might submerge her in the battle of the labels, and smilingly but vigorously dissented.

The peculiar glow in her eyes, which eighty-two years and two cataract operations had not dimmed, the piercing kindness which enveloped you from the moment you came into her presence, and which reached out over the telephone wires or in an airmail pouch, the readiness with the Word of God, and the immediacy of the excuse for any failing mentioned in her hearing—there were these and a hundred other signs that she was a holy woman, but such an observation would not twice have been made in her presence. On the first occasion it would have been impaled on stilletto-like wit, which could deflate all pietism and pomposity—without hurting. You would just know better than to try again.

Some gifted pen—Sister Bertrande's, I hope—should be put immediately to the writing of Sister Catherine Sullivan's life. The Daughters of Charity, St. Louis province, owe it to us all to set before us workers-at-formation, our own and others, a picture of what a near-ideal American nun was and perennially may be. Meanwhile, for those of us who knew her, it may sound like an exaggeration but it is not, to say that the whole world is a drearier place with Sister Catherine in Heaven. But it will be fun, some day, to learn how she is taking them by storm up there.

Sister Mary Emil, I.H.M.

173

In life, especially when she was most active and vigorous, Sister Catherine could not enter a room, or an auditorium, where heads did not turn, and feet make a beeline to be near her, just to have a word with her. Sisters, seeing her for the first time, would say: "You can tell she loves Sisters; I did not feel like a stranger in pressing her hand, I felt that she sort of belonged to me."

So, with Sister Mary Emil, one can readily wonder if St. Peter had to call for order when she appeared at the pearly gates. But nothing, I firmly believe, can divert her attention from those she loved and left still plodding the uphill way she so magnificently lighted for hearts that were weary and steps that were faltering. These have a special claim on her now. As in life, so in eternity, she will not fail them; for now more than ever she can be truly everywhere. And wherever Sister Catherine is it is always Springtime.